AMERICAN HORTICULTURAL SOCIETY
PRACTICAL GUIDES

PRUNING
& TRAINING

AMERICAN HORTICULTURAL SOCIETY
PRACTICAL GUIDES

PRUNING
& TRAINING

LIN HAWTHORNE

DK Publishing

LONDON, NEW YORK, MUNICH,
MELBOURNE, and DELHI

PROJECT EDITOR Lin Hawthorne
ART EDITOR Martin Hendry
US EDITOR Ray Rogers

SERIES EDITOR Helen Fewster
SERIES ART EDITOR Ursula Dawson
MANAGING EDITOR Anna Kruger
MANAGING ART EDITOR Lee Griffiths
DTP DESIGNER Louise Waller
PRODUCTION MANAGER Mandy Inness

First American Edition, 2003
00 01 02 03 04 05 10 9 8 7 6 5 4 3 2 1

Published in the United States by
DK Publishing, Inc.
375 Hudson Street
New York, New York 10014

Copyright © 2003 Dorling Kindersley Limited, London

Library of Congress Cataloging-in-Publication data is available
from the Library of Congress.
ISBN 0–7894–9482–5

Reproduced by Colourscan, Singapore
Printed and bound by TBB, Slovakia

See our complete catalog at
www.dk.com

CONTENTS

PRUNING AND TRAINING

WHY PRUNE?

PRUNING AND TRAINING AIM TO ENSURE that plants are as vigorous and healthy as possible, at the least risk of infection by disease, and free of structural weakness. It can also create striking plant features by enhancing ornamental qualities such as bark, flowers, foliage, and fruit. Since pruning always causes some stress, it is important never to prune without a specific benefit in mind or without a clear idea of the effect of every pruning cut you make.

MAINTAINING FORM AND EFFECT

One good reason for pruning is to ensure a well-shaped specimen that is strong and healthy and that displays its most desirable features to its greatest effect. For example, many trees grow naturally with a single leading shoot and an evenly distributed network of branches above a clear trunk. Many trees need little pruning to achieve their natural form, but if they develop two leaders, this must be remedied as soon as possible if the tree is to be structurally sound at maturity (*see p.27*). In some plants the most desirable feature is their variegated foliage. This sometimes reverts to plain green (*see p.39*), and this, too, must be dealt with promptly if the variegation is to be maintained.

GOOD PARTNERS
To create good partnerships, it is essential to know how and when to prune both of them. Here, Clematis 'Nelly Moser' climbs through the rose Dublin Bay.

◀ Acer pseudoplatanus *'Brilliantissimum' naturally forms a shapely crown.*

PRUNING FOR HEALTH

In many cases, pruning to maintain good health simply involves the removal of dead, damaged, or diseased shoots. Most plants have some ability to limit the spread of disease, and the aim of pruning should be to assist a return to perfect health. Dead wood is removed because it has the potential to harbor infections that may spread to living tissue. Removing damaged wood assists recovery by minimizing the risk of disease-causing organisms entering the wound. If tissue is already diseased, cutting back to healthy, living wood helps limit further spread of the disease.

Ragged wound may allow wood-rotting organisms to enter

Cutting back to a strong bud encourages healthy new growth

DAMAGED BRANCH
A torn, broken stem with jagged tissue and ripped bark provides ideal conditions for the entry of diseases and must be dealt with promptly.

DEAD PATCHES
Fungal diseases proliferate in dead tissue and may spread. Once removed, any gaps can be disguised by tying living shoots across the hole.

Some fungi have the ability to spread rapidly down the stem into living tissue

Affected growth is cut back well into healthy living tissue that shows no signs of infection

DISEASED WOOD
Cutting away diseased tissue by making a neat, clean cut with sharp pruners creates a small wound that the plant is usually able to repair rapidly.

NIP IN THE BUD

Don't wait until normal pruning time to deal with dead, diseased, or damaged growth. Prompt action prevents more deterioration.

◀ FROST DAMAGE
When cutting frost-damaged growth back to live wood, it is best to wait until danger of further frost has passed to avoid exposing new growth to further damage.

PRUNING AND TRAINING FOR PRODUCTIVITY

Growing and training plants on a wall or other support makes a very useful and decorative contribution to the garden. The trained plant takes up less space, can hide an unsightly wall or fence, and, in many cases, it increases their productivity, too.

Training stems to the horizontal breaks the dominance of the main, vertical shoots, causing them to produce sideshoots (*see pp.10–11*). In many plants, especially those in the rose family, such as roses, flowering quince (*Chaenomeles*), and cotoneasters, these sideshoots produce significantly more flowers and fruit.

WALL-TRAINED PYRACANTHA
The naturally arching stems of pyracanthas are particularly suited to horizontal training, producing more flowers and fruit as a result.

Pruning for Flowering

There are several techniques that can be used to enhance a plant's decorative value. Pruning to increase the size or the number of flowers, often the most ornamental feature, is one of the most usual.

At its simplest, it may mean pruning out old wood to promote the growth of strong new shoots that flower more abundantly (*see pp.41–42*). Spur pruning (*see right*) is a little more sophisticated. Shortening the sideshoots often encourages more flower-buds to form on so-called flowering spurs.

SHORTENING SIDESHOOTS
Unpruned Chaenomeles *stems bear few flowers. Cutting back sideshoots to 2–3 buds to form spurs induces profuse flowering.*

Unpruned sideshoots bear few flowers

Sideshoots pruned back to 2–3 buds

Ornamental and Special Effects

Several pruning and training methods are used for purely ornamental purposes. Topiary is an art that has long been used to shape plants in formal, geometric, or more whimsical forms. Pinch-pruning is used to induce bushy growth and can be adapted to produce spectacular foliage or flower displays in many different shapes. Some plants respond to hard pruning by producing larger, more colorful leaves.

Each time a growing tip is pinched out, the stem branches, so growth becomes more dense and compact

PINCH-PRUNING
The dense lollipop head of this standard coleus is formed by pinching out the growing tips of each shoot between finger and thumb.

SPECIAL-EFFECT PLANTS

For topiary: Bay (*Laurus nobilis*), barberries (*Berberis*), boxwood (*Buxus sempervirens*), *Cupressus sempervirens*, hollies (*Ilex*), *Osmanthus*, privets (*Ligustrum* sp.), *Prunus lusitanica*, yews (*Taxus*).

For pinch pruning: *Argyranthemum*, coleus, chrysanthemums, fuchsias, *Helichrysum petiolare*, geraniums (*Pelargonium*).

For foliage enhancement: *Acer negundo* 'Flamingo', *Catalpa bignonioides*, *Cotinus coggygria*, *Eucalyptus*, *Paulownia*, *Sambucus*.

Shoots may reach 8ft (2.5m) in a single season and make a wonderful architectural focal point

The soft, downy leaves grow much larger and with richer color, especially if fertilized after pruning

► TOPIARY FORMS
This sculptural spiral has been created and is maintained by regular close clipping. Plants for topiary must have dense, pliable growth that is able to withstand frequent pruning.

◄ FOLIAGE EFFECT
Extra-large, tropical-looking leaves are your reward for cutting Paulownia *back hard every year. This is also a way of growing some trees as very ornamental container plants.*

HOW PRUNING WORKS

ONE KEY FEATURE OF PRUNING IS THAT if material is removed from a plant or a stem tied down to the horizontal, the plant's usual response is to make new growth elsewhere. Knowing this, you can prune to induce growth where it is wanted and vary the quantity, direction, and vigor of growth at will. You should assess the entire plant before making any cuts, but, since all pruning causes a degree of stress to a plant, you should never cut without good reason.

REMOVING THE SHOOT TIP

Plants produce hormones in the topmost stem tip – the "apical" tip – that suppress branching lower down to ensure that stems grow straight up toward the sunlight they need to make food. If the main stem tip is cut out, this suppression is reduced, and buds lower down the stem begin to branch out. This is known as breaking apical dominance; it is the principle behind all pruning cuts that are made to promote branching, bushy growth.

With the shoot tip intact, the stem grows strongly upward toward the light

Buds that would form branches are suppressed

The shoot tip has been removed, so the bud below grows out strongly

Suppression of lower buds is reduced, and branching begins

SMALL IS BEAUTIFUL
• Cutting or pinching out shoot tips when plants are still small ensures that they begin branching from low down at an early age. This means shrubs develop dense, bushy growth; it can also result in the formation of a multistemmed tree.
• It is best to make pruning wounds as small as possible; the smaller the wounded area, the lower the risk of infection. Small wounds heal more easily and quickly than large ones, and the risk of scarring is also minimized.

INDUCING BRANCHING
If the main stem tip is removed, the next bud down assumes dominance and starts to grow strongly. But its dominance is not absolute, so lower buds can also grow out.

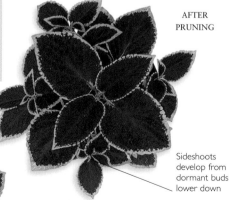

AFTER
PRUNING

Leaves lower down on the stem have dormant buds in the leaf axils (the junction at which the leaf joins the stem)

BEFORE
PRUNING

Sideshoots develop from dormant buds lower down

The shoot tip concentrates all of its energy into growing upward and suppresses branching lower down

PRUNING FOR BUSHY GROWTH
This coleus clearly shows the effect of removing the shoot tip. New shoots have been stimulated into growth by its removal, creating dense, bushy growth.

MAXIMIZING FLOWERS AND FRUIT

Bending and tying a vertical stem to the horizontal has a similar effect to removing the shoot tip, reducing its dominance and allowing the plant's lower buds to branch out. Instead of growing relentlessly upward, the stem produces sideshoots along its length, and these are more likely to bear flowers or fruits.

You can use this technique when wall training climbers or other flexible-stemmed plants. It ensures good coverage and an even distribution of flowers and fruits.

VERTICAL STEM
This unpruned climbing rose stem and sideshoot will grow upward to produce a leggy plant with all of its flowers near the top and possibly out of sight.

Strong upward growth

Sideshoot also grows vertically upward if left to its own devices

HORIZONTAL STEM
A horizontal stem bears flowering sideshoots of almost equal vigor along its length, with the potential of bringing them down to eye level.

Sideshoot tied to the horizontal

Flower-bearing shoots branch out

SURVIVING DAMAGE AND DISEASE

Many woody plants can limit the spread of disease by forming a natural chemical barrier to isolate diseased tissue from the main body of the plant. In response to wounding, the plant can transport chemicals to the wound site to prevent the entry of disease. Scar tissue, or "callus," grows over the wound to form an air- and watertight seal. So when making pruning cuts, aim to reinforce the plant's own natural defenses.

STEM DIEBACK
A natural barrier halts the dieback of a stub left by poor pruning. Dormant buds beneath the cut will produce new growth.

Distinct natural barrier between living and dead wood

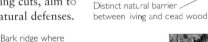

Dieback caused by incorrect pruning

Cut straight across the demarcation line

Bark ridge where branch and trunk meet

Cutting here does not breach plant's defenses

Natural chemicals flow into here (the branch collar) in response to wounding

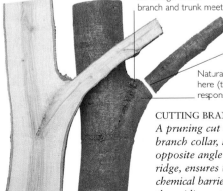

CUTTING BRANCHES
A pruning cut outside the branch collar, at an equal and opposite angle to the bark ridge, ensures that the plant's chemical barrier remains intact, thus aiding rapid healing.

AFTER PRUNING
With a cut made just beyond the branch collar, the plant can seal the wound with a protective callus of scar tissue.

RESPONSES TO PRUNING

In general, light pruning results in limited regrowth, and hard pruning produces more vigorous regrowth, provided the plant is healthy and can tolerate hard pruning. Pruning too hard too often, however, may eventually weaken the plant. It's always best to choose the plant to fit the space so that you don't have to repeatedly trim to fit.

Timing of pruning is critical. Pruning evergreens too early in spring or too late in summer induces soft, new growth that may be damaged by cold or wind. Pruning at the wrong time also risks removing the coming season's flowers (*see box, above right*).

CHECK BEFORE CUTTING

- Have a clear aim in mind before making any cuts to ensure that the cuts you make give the desired results. For example, do you wish to induce bushy growth or strong new regrowth, or to produce more flower shoots?
- Ascertain the correct pruning time. As a rule of thumb, plants that flower before midsummer are pruned after flowering. Those that flower after midsummer are pruned in late winter or early spring.

The head is kept neat and bushy by pruning lightly to shape after flowering

THE NATURAL STATE
The natural habit of Syringa meyeri *is to grow as a densely branched, bushy shrub clothed with branches to ground level. It bears its flowers in late spring and early summer and is pruned lightly after the flowers have faded.*

A TRAINED STANDARD
Because it responds well to pruning, Syringa meyeri *can also easily be trained and pruned to form a free-flowering, mophead standard on a clear stem.*

The stem is kept clear of branches by pinching or rubbing out new shoots that arise below the head

Healthy growth is maintained by growing in a fertile soil mix and by regularly fertilizing and watering

TO PRUNE OR NOT TO PRUNE

Plants that respond well to hard pruning:
Aucuba japonica, barberries (most), *Buddleja* and cultivars, *Buxus sempervirens*, *Caryopteris* cultivars, *Catalpa bignonioides*, *Chaenomeles* cultivars, *Choisya ternata*, *Cornus alba*, *C. stolonifera*, *C. sanguinea*, *Cotinus coggygria*, *Elaeagnus* sp. and cultivars, *Eucalyptus* (most), *Ilex* (hollies, most), *Laurus nobilis* (bay), *Paulownia tomentosa*, *Phlomis fruticosa*, *Rosa* (roses, most), *Salix* (willows, most), *Syringa* (lilacs, most).

Plants that need minimal or no pruning:
Arbutus (strawberry trees), camellias, *Carya* (hickories), *Cercidiphyllum japonicum* (katsura tree), *Cladrastis*, *Cornus kousa* and other flowering dogwoods, *Daphne*, *Eucryphia*, *Fremontodendron californicum*, *Halesia*, *Hamamelis* (witch hazels), *Juglans* (walnuts, most), *Kalopanax septemlobus*, *Koelreuteria paniculata*, *Parrotia persica*, *Platycarya strobilacea*, *Rhus verniciflua*, *Sophora*, *Styrax*.

DIFFERENT HABIT, SAME GENUS

Botanical classification places plants into a genus according to shared characteristics, such as flower form and petal number. Plants within a group, or genus, share some characteristics, but this doesn't necessarily mean they all look exactly alike. Don't assume that all plants that share a genus respond in the same way to pruning. They often do, but they may vary in the way they grow; see the honeysuckles below. Form and flowering time – two major factors to be considered when choosing suitable pruning techniques – are different. Be aware that plants may also vary in their tolerance of pruning: one may be stimulated by hard pruning; another may die of shock.

LONICERA JAPONICA
A climbing, twining plant with long, slender stems and an abundance of flowers, typical of a genus commonly known as honeysuckle.

LONICERA NITIDA 'BAGGESEN'S GOLD'
A nonclimbing, shrubby honeysuckle with a dense habit and small, glossy leaves, this evergreen is often used as a hedging plant.

FERTILIZE AND MULCH FOR NEW GROWTH

Many pruning cuts remove actively growing shoots and so deprive the plant of energy-producing tissue. At the same time, energy demands are increased by stimulating abundant flowering or fruiting. If a plant is to remain healthy (rather than be stressed) by pruning, it must have sufficient nutrients and water to produce replacement growth.

Apply a complete fertilizer to moist soil around the base of the plant in spring, then follow with a mulch of organic matter. If repeat applications are needed, do not apply after midsummer – late, soft growth will be vulnerable to cold damage.

MULCH AFTER FERTILIZING
Apply a mulch, 3in (8cm) deep and avoiding the immediate stem base, to help retain soil moisture and reduce competition from weeds.

HOW TO CUT CORRECTLY

PRUNING CUTS SHOULD ALWAYS BE as small, clean, and neat as you can make them, bearing in mind that you want the plant to heal as rapidly as possible. They should also be made with clean, sharp tools. The younger the wood, the faster it heals, so try to prune young shoots before they become hard and woody, and twigs before they become branches. The larger the wound, the more opportunity disease has to enter, especially if the wounds are ragged or bruised.

MAKING CUTS

A woody plant's natural defenses are strongest at the branch collar (a swelling where the branch meets the trunk), at a fork on the branch, or at a bud or leaf joint (a node). Making small, clean cuts at these points helps speed healing; make them the sites of first choice for pruning cuts.

CLEAN, SHARP, SAFE

• Keep your pruning tools clean to reduce the risk of spreading diseases from plant to plant in the sap on their blades.
• Keep your pruning tools sharp so that they cut cleanly without bruising or tearing. This also reduces the strain on their mechanism and on your own hands, wrists, and arms.

▶ GOOD AND BAD CUTS
A gently sloping cut is preferable, because rain cannot gather on a sloping surface. Water is a prime carrier of disease; many wood-rotting fungi spread by spores washed from the air in raindrops and in splashes from nearby plants.

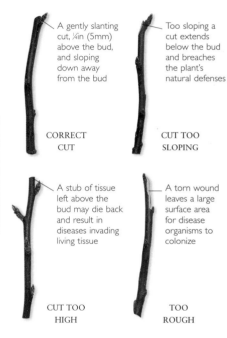

A gently slanting cut, ¼in (5mm) above the bud, and sloping down away from the bud

CORRECT CUT

Too sloping a cut extends below the bud and breaches the plant's natural defenses

CUT TOO SLOPING

A stub of tissue left above the bud may die back and result in diseases invading living tissue

CUT TOO HIGH

A torn wound leaves a large surface area for disease organisms to colonize

TOO ROUGH

BUD ARRANGEMENTS

Woody plants produce buds in one of two main patterns, and this needs to be taken into account when making pruning cuts. Alternate buds arise at intervals on different sides of the stem. With these, it is possible to make the preferred sloping cut, from which a single new shoot will grow. Opposite buds arise in pairs at the same point on the stem. A sloping cut would damage one or both of the buds, so a neat, straight cut above the bud is the only option. Two new shoots will arise from the buds.

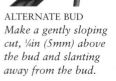

One new shoot will grow from the bud below the cut

Two new shoots will grow from the buds below the cut

ALTERNATE BUD
Make a gently sloping cut, ¼in (5mm) above the bud and slanting away from the bud.

OPPOSITE BUD
Make a cut squarely across the shoot, ¼in (5mm) above a pair of healthy buds.

LARGER CUTS

It is sometimes inevitable that large pruning cuts will need to be made, as when cutting off the branch of a tree. They often take several seasons to heal, leaving potential entry points for wood-rotting diseases.

In this case, it is imperative to make cuts that will heal with maximum speed. Make a smooth cut at the right point – where the plant's natural defenses are strongest – then scar tissue or callus will grow from the edge to the center, gradually sealing the wound and preventing entry of harmful organisms.

Make a cut just beyond the branch collar, which can be seen as a slight swelling between branch and trunk

For thick wood, always use a powerful tool, such as these strong, sharp loppers

USING WOUND PAINTS

It is best to avoid using wound paints. Wound paints were once applied to cuts to provide an artificial barrier to infection, but they are not very helpful and some may even hinder the healing process. Exposed tissue is never sterile, and some microorganisms are present (but dormant) beneath the bark, becoming active only when the bark is damaged. These harmful organisms become trapped beneath the paint. Such paints can also kill beneficial microorganisms that can inhibit wood-rotting ones.

BRANCH COLLAR
In response to the cut, the tree sends natural disinfecting chemicals to the branch collar, isolating the wound from the sap flow up the main trunk, so diseases cannot spread to the main body of the tree.

PROTECTIVE CALLUS
A clean cut allows healing to proceed naturally. Callus tissue will eventually seal the wound to make it completely air- and watertight.

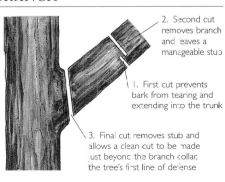

ROUGH CUT
A jagged wound that breached the branch collar allowed fungal spores to invade and begin rotting the main trunk. The rot may eventually kill the tree.

HOW TO SAW OFF A LARGER BRANCH

You should remove only branches that are no higher than shoulder height and that are light enough for you to support. For your own safety, any major pruning that needs to be done from a ladder or that involves large branches should be done by a professional arborist. Make a first cut (the undercut) about 12in (30cm) from the trunk, beneath the branch. Make a second cut (the top cut) just beyond and above the undercut, cutting squarely until the branch falls away. The final cut is made just beyond the branch collar.

2. Second cut removes branch and leaves a manageable stub

1. First cut prevents bark from tearing and extending into the trunk

3. Final cut removes stub and allows a clean cut to be made just beyond the branch collar, the tree's first line of defense

TOOLS AND EQUIPMENT

IT IS ALWAYS WELL WORTH INVESTING in the best tools you can afford and, ideally, to have a special tool for every task. If well cared-for, high-quality tools can last a lifetime. The right tool for the job always gives the best result, and this is especially true of cutting tools. Before you buy new tools, check that they feel comfortable to use, that they fit your hand well and are easy to grip, and that you can use them without strain.

TOOLS FOR THE JOB

The basic tools required for pruning work are pruners and, for heavier work, a pair of loppers or a long-handled tree pruner. Thick branches are best cut with a saw; a pruning saw is easy to manipulate between closely spaced branches. Use a pruning knife with a large, downswept blade to neaten snags. Wear heavy-duty gloves or gauntlets to protect your hands and wrists, especially if pruning thorny plants.

Hand shears are easy to control when clipping hedges or other plants and are best for topiary work. A power trimmer is ideal for large hedges, and a nylon-line trimmer makes short work of groundcovers. Wear goggles when using power tools.

Sharp steel cutting blade makes a precise, clean cut

Molded grip is comfortable to use

PRUNERS

LOPPERS

Long handles give extra reach and leverage, and buffers prevent jarring when operating

The hook is lowered over the branch to be cut, then the blade is operated by a lever system

PROTECTIVE GOGGLES

PRUNING KNIFE

TREE PRUNER

HAND SHEARS

THE BEST TOOLS
The steel blades of most good-quality cutting tools are easy to sharpen. The blades can be removed when damaged or blunted and then either reground or replaced.

PRUNING SAW

PROTECTIVE GLOVES

TOOL CARE

- Always keep the cutting blades sharp.
- Clean and dry tools after use. Wipe with an oily rag to keep blades in good condition and free of rust.
- Use tools only for the purpose for which they were designed. Don't attempt to cut shoots or branches that exceed their capabilities.
- Never use pruners for cutting wire unless they have a wire-cutting notch.

USING TOOLS CORRECTLY

A pruning saw cuts only on the pull stroke, and its teeth are arranged to not clog up when cutting green wood. Straight and curved bladed models are available. Both are easy to maneuver in confined spaces. Use a pruning saw to remove thick, woody growth or dead stubs from the base of rose bushes, or to thin old, knobby systems of flowering spurs if they become overcrowded.

A pruning knife is handy for nipping out soft growth tips and for smoothing rough cuts. Don't use it to cut string, it blunts the blade.

USING POWER TOOLS

• Tools that use electricity must be fitted with a circuit breaker to protect you should you accidentally cut through the cord.
• Never work alone when using a power hedge trimmer.
• Never trim wet plants or work in wet, windy, or snowy weather.
• Protective goggles should always be worn when using power tools. Ear protection in the form of ear plugs or mufflers is also strongly recommended.

A curved pruning saw is perfectly designed for tight spots

◄ USING A PRUNING SAW
The narrow blade of a pruning saw makes it possible to cut out stubs of dead wood without damaging live stems.

► USING A KNIFE
Use a sharp knife to neaten any rough edges on a ragged pruning cut.

The curved blade of a pruning knife gives greater control

HOW TO USE PRUNERS

You can use pruners for all soft growth and for stems up to about ½in (1cm) in diameter without undue strain. Use them the right way up – that is, the sharp cutting blade should be nearer to the bud or stem that you are cutting. In this way, the crushing effect of the thicker blade is confined to the stem you are removing.

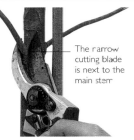

The narrow cutting blade is next to the main stem

CORRECT USE

Thicker blade is closer to the stem being retained

INCORRECT USE

HOW TO USE LOPPERS

Loppers are used for thicker stems up to 1in (2.5cm) or so in diameter. If the stem fits entirely within the bite of the loppers, the extra leverage of the handles will make cutting almost effortless without any undue strain on the blades. As with pruners, the sharp cutting blade should be next to the main stem.

Stem fits easily within the jaws of the loppers, giving a neat, clean cut

CORRECT USE

Too big a stem strains the blades, and crushing or tearing of tissue is likely

INCORRECT USE

ORNAMENTAL TREES

THE AIMS OF PRUNING

AS THE LONGEST-LIVED AND MOST structurally important elements in the garden, the trees that you plant will form an enduring legacy if properly trained when young. Most trees need little pruning once established, but early pruning and training aim to create a strong and well-balanced tree that remains safe and healthy well into maturity. Forming a sound branch structure will also help display the tree's ornamental virtues at their best.

WHEN AND WHEN NOT TO PRUNE

The timing of pruning is important: for most trees, it is usually best done in winter, when the tree is fully dormant. In nature, this is the time when a tree is most likely to suffer injury from snow, ice, or wind. The tree is usually able to heal its wounds naturally when new growth begins in spring. Most trees, however, tolerate light pruning to correct localized problems at any time of year. The exceptions are trees such as birches and walnuts, which "bleed" sap from pruning wounds made when the sap is rising in late winter, or when the tree is in leaf between spring and midsummer. Some trees, such as cherries, are susceptible to diseases at certain times of year; these are usually pruned in summer.

LIGHT AND AIRY
The golden-leaved Robinia pseudoacacia 'Frisia' is best pruned in mid- to late summer, because it becomes more susceptible to infection by wood-rotting fungi if pruned in winter.

◀ TRUE COLORS *Young foliage tints of* Populus × jackii *'Aurora' are enhanced by regular pruning.*

BUYING YOUNG TREES

ALTHOUGH YOU CAN BUY already-trained trees of three, four, or more years of age, it is usually better value to begin, if possible, with a small, sturdy young specimen of one or two years old. The larger a tree upon purchase, the slower it is to establish and the more post-planting aftercare it needs if it is to grow well. There is so much more pleasure to be gained in watching a tree that you have grown and trained from infancy develop to healthy maturity.

THE CORRECT TRAINING

Training a young tree begins in the first year after germination. The aim is to ensure that the main stem grows from a single leading bud at its tip so that it forms a straight trunk. In the first few years, it will also develop side branches (*see feathered trees, p.22*) whose leaves help produce the thickening growth of the main stem. As the tree grows, the side branches are usually selectively pruned to produce a clear trunk.

The developing root system is very important, too. It must have enough room in the pot to grow without constriction if it is to develop in proportion to the top-growth it sustains. The tree's spread should not be more than three or four times the width of its pot.

The single main shoot is well clothed with side branches and a full a complement of healthy leaves

Stem is secured to a lightweight stake that extends above the growing tip; new growth is tied in as it grows

WELL-TRAINED EXAMPLE
As it completes its first growing season, this young tree is upright, strong, and healthy. The pot is big enough to hold enough unconstricted roots to sustain the top-growth.

DANGER POINTS

• Young trees with inadequate roots are likely to suffer shock after planting, because the roots cannot provide enough nutrition for the new top-growth. They are unlikely to grow well and will probably suffer dieback of the growing shoots. If the top-growth is too extensive, the only remedy is to prune to redress the balance of roots to shoots.

• Always choose young trees with a single, well-supported main stem with a healthy growing point at the tip. If there are side branches, they should be evenly distributed around the main stem. If a tree has been allowed to develop more than one leading shoot, it is likely to produce narrowly forked branches that become structurally unsafe at maturity. The remedy is to select a strong, new leading shoot and prune to remove any nearby shoots that compete with it.

Top-growth is too extensive to be sustained by a rootball that is constricted in too small a pot

Stem has grown lopsided without the support of a stake and has been allowed to develop two leading shoots

NEGLECTED EXAMPLE
Without remedial pruning, this neglected young tree stands little chance of developing into a sturdy and well-shaped specimen at maturity.

GRAFTED TREES

Many ornamental trees are propagated by grafting a bud, or a length of stem, of a desirable cultivar onto a suitable rootstock. The point at which the two tissues join is known as the graft union. It may be seen as a slight swelling at the base of the trunk on "bottom-grafted" trees. The tree will grow from a grafted bud as a single shoot. If a length of stem has been grafted, the top-most bud will form the new leading or main shoot. Any growth from the rootstock or from the stem below the graft point must be removed as seen. On "top-grafted" trees, usually weeping standards (*see p.24*), buds are grafted at the top of a clear stem.

Shoot from the topmost bud will grow out to extend the length of the main stem

Graft union protected with tape

Any growth from below the graft union will be of the stock plant and must be removed

YOUNG GRAFTED TREE
A newly grafted young plant should be staked to keep it growing straight and to protect it from breakage at the graft point until tissue is fully fused.

POT-GROWN AND BARE-ROOT TREES

If you choose to buy a partially trained tree, try to select it in person and check for potential problems before buying. Transport it carefully under cover or under wraps; stems and buds suffer stress and are likely to be damaged if transported on an open roof rack. If bare-root plants are exposed to air and wind, the fine roots will dry out and die. The roots of trees do not usually need pruning upon transplanting, but if any are damaged, prune them away cleanly before planting. Shorten coiled, overly long, or lopsided roots to leave a good spread of roots emanating from the main stem.

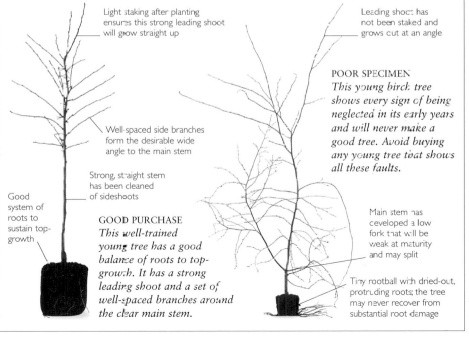

Light staking after planting ensures this strong leading shoot will grow straight up

Well-spaced side branches form the desirable wide angle to the main stem

Strong, straight stem has been cleaned of sideshoots

Good system of roots to sustain top-growth

GOOD PURCHASE
This well-trained young tree has a good balance of roots to top-growth. It has a strong leading shoot and a set of well-spaced branches around the clear main stem.

Leading shoot has not been staked and grows cut at an angle

POOR SPECIMEN
This young birch tree shows every sign of being neglected in its early years and will never make a good tree. Avoid buying any young tree that shows all these faults.

Main stem has developed a low fork that will be weak at maturity and may split

Tiny rootball with dried-out, protruding roots; the tree may never recover from substantial root damage

TRAINING TREE FORMS

O NCE A YOUNG TREE HAS BEEN planted out, training can continue while it is growing in its permanent site. In the first year, most trees grow a single main shoot and produce branches in the second year. Training begins in the second or third winter. Trees are pruned and trained in a variety of forms, but it's best to choose one that is most like the form the tree develops naturally, because this is the most likely to remain structurally sound into maturity.

FEATHERED TREES

Most trees have this form when young and shed their lower branches naturally as they mature. It is by far the easiest form to produce, since it requires little pruning other than the removal of crossing, dead, diseased, or damaged wood. It is especially suitable for *Cornus alternifolia, C. capitata,* and *Malus.* Many evergreens, such as hollies (*Ilex*), *Eucryphia,* and most conifers, however, naturally retain this neat, conical form and need the barest minimum of pruning to keep the shape well into maturity. The formative pruning of feathered evergreens is done after late summer and before midwinter. Deciduous trees are pruned when dormant.

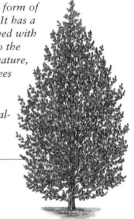

FEATHERED TREE
This is the natural form of most young trees. It has a central trunk clothed with branches almost to the ground. As they mature, most deciduous trees shed their lower branches and develop into central-leader standards.

Side branches are evenly spaced all around the main trunk

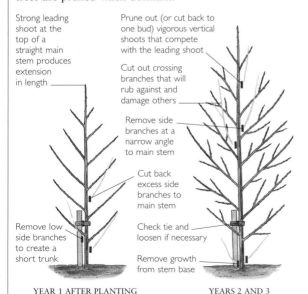

Strong leading shoot at the top of a straight main stem produces extension in length

Prune out (or cut back to one bud) vigorous vertical shoots that compete with the leading shoot

Cut out crossing branches that will rub against and damage others

Remove side branches at a narrow angle to main stem

Cut back excess side branches to main stem

Remove low side branches to create a short trunk

Check tie and loosen if necessary

Remove growth from stem base

YEAR 1 AFTER PLANTING   YEARS 2 AND 3

WELL TRAINED

Side branches that make a narrow angle to the main stem should be removed first. If they are allowed to develop, they may grow into heavy branches with a narrow junction between the trunk and branch that is likely to become structurally weak at maturity.

PRUNING FEATHERED TREES
Cut off any side branches that are not well spaced or positioned to maintain a well-balanced shape. If side branches grow more strongly on one side, tip-prune the weaker shoots on the other side to stimulate growth.

CENTRAL-LEADER STANDARDS

Many trees take this form naturally; as they mature, lower branches die back as they are shaded out by an increasingly dense crown. But in order to create this attractive form from a young age, the lower branches can be cleared from a feathered tree. The aim of pruning and training is to maintain the strong growth of a central leading shoot and to create a clear trunk. Side branches aid the growth in girth of a strong, tapered trunk and are removed over several years. If they are removed all at once, dormant buds lower on the trunk are stimulated into growth, which inhibits top-growth.

CENTRAL-LEADER TREE
This example has a distinct leading shoot and a straight stem with a symmetrical crown of branches atop a clear stem of 6ft (2m) or more.

Side branches are removed to clear the stem when young and small so that they leave minimal scarring

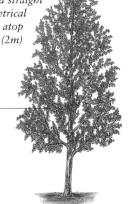

POPULAR EXAMPLES

TALL (over 70ft/20m)
Aesculus hippocastanum,
  horse chestnut
Liquidambar styaciflua,
  sweetgum
Quercus petraea, sessile oak

MEDIUM (30–70ft/10–20m)
Alnus incana
Carpinus betulus 'Fastigiata'
Catalpa bignonioides

Corylus colurna
Davidia involucrata
Malus tschonoskii
Paulownia tomentosa

SMALL (to 30ft/10m)
Laburnum anagyroides
Prunus maackii
Prunus serrula
Sorbus cashmiriana
Sorbus hupehensis

PRUNING CENTRAL-LEADER STANDARDS
To remove side branches make cuts that do not breach the branch collar (see p.11); if the swelling is invisible, leave a stub of no more than ¼in (5mm). If the leader is lost or overtaken by another shoot, train in a replacement (see p.27).

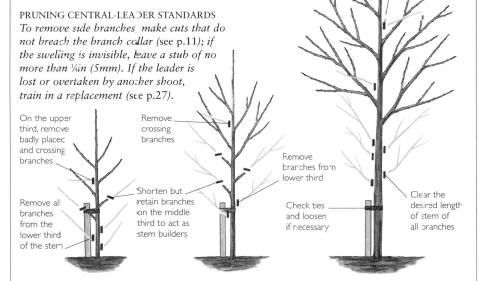

Leading shoot continues to grow strongly

As the crown develops, remove crossing branches to avoid congestion

On the upper third, remove badly placed and crossing branches

Remove crossing branches

Remove branches from lower third

Remove all branches from the lower third of the stem

Shorten but retain branches on the middle third to act as stem builders

Check ties and loosen if necessary

Clear the desired length of stem of all branches

YEAR 1 AFTER PLANTING

YEARS 2 AND 3

YEAR 4

BRANCHED-HEAD STANDARD

Branched-head standards do occur in nature, since the leading shoot may gradually begin to lose dominance with age, but pruning to produce the form is often done on trees that would otherwise grow to considerable heights. Training in the first and second years is the same as for central-leader standards (*see p.23*).

BRANCHED-HEAD TREES	
Acer saccharum	Fraxinus americana
Catalpa bignonioides	Koelreuteria
Celtis occidentalis	Malus (Crabapple)
Cornus kousa	Prunus × yedoensis
Crataegus (Hawthorn)	Styrax obassia
Eucommia ulmoides	Tilia tomentosa

PRUNING BRANCHED-HEAD TREES
When 3–4 strong branches have developed above the required height of the clear trunk, the leading shoot is removed to create a branched head.

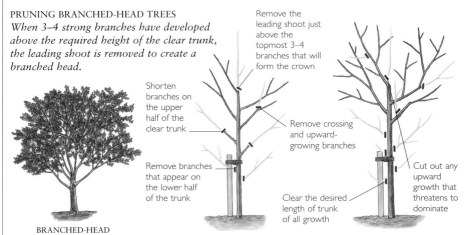

Remove the leading shoot just above the topmost 3–4 branches that will form the crown

Shorten branches on the upper half of the clear trunk

Remove branches that appear on the lower half of the trunk

Remove crossing and upward-growing branches

Clear the desired length of trunk of all growth

Cut out any upward growth that threatens to dominate

BRANCHED-HEAD STANDARD

YEAR 3 OR 4, WINTER

YEAR 4 OR 5, WINTER

WEEPING STANDARDS

Some naturally weeping trees can be trained into this form, but weeping standards are produced mostly by top-grafting several buds on top of a clear stem. It's a form that often needs pruning throughout its life to avoid congestion in the crown. Congestion leads to a buildup of dead wood and debris that is unsightly and may harbor disease. Staking, often with a tall stake to the head of the tree, is often needed for some years after the head develops.

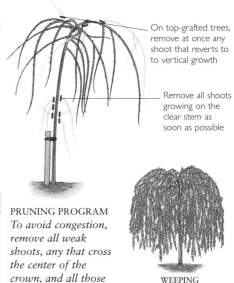

On top-grafted trees, remove at once any shoot that reverts to to vertical growth

Remove all shoots growing on the clear stem as soon as possible

WEEPING TREES	
Betula pendula 'Youngii'	Prunus × subhirtella 'Pendula'
Fraxinus excelsior 'Pendula'	Pyrus salicifolia 'Pendula'
Malus 'Red Jade'	Sophora japonica 'Pendula'
Morus alba 'Pendula'	

PRUNING PROGRAM
To avoid congestion, remove all weak shoots, any that cross the center of the crown, and all those that grow upward.

WEEPING STANDARD

MULTISTEMMED TREES

Pruning a tree to a multistemmed form is an ideal way of bringing a treelike presence to a small garden and ensures great value in trees with ornamental bark. Some trees, such as *Celtis australis*, struggle to maintain a central leader in areas where summers are cool but are equally attractive as a multi-stemmed trees. It is the natural form of many trees that produce suckers from their base or branch low down, but pruning enhances this effect by controlling the number and spacing of the trunks.

MULTISTEMMED TREE
Branching low down at or near ground level, this form develops several distinct stems or trunks and often resembles a large, bushy shrub.

GOOD CHOICES

Acacia dealbata	*C. siliquastrum*
Acer pensylvanicum	*Cotinus obovatus*
Amelanchier	*Halesia*
Betula nigra	*Maackia amurensis*
B. pendula	*Nyssa sylvatica*
Cercidiphyllum	*Oxydendrum*
japonicum	*arboreum*
Cercis chinensis,	*Viburnum sieboldii*

FROM A SINGLE STEM

To create a multi-stemmed tree from a single stem, the stem is cut back almost to ground level, and the resulting shoots are thinned to create a well-spaced framework of low branches.

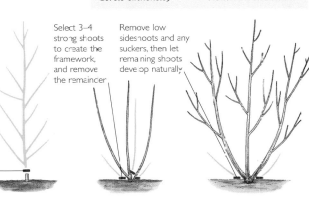

Cut back the stem of a two-year-old tree to a strong bud at about 3in (8cm) above ground level

Select 3–4 strong shoots to create the framework, and remove the remainder

Remove low sideshoots and any suckers, then let remaining shoots develop naturally

YEAR 1, WINTER   YEAR 2, WINTER   YEAR 3, WINTER

ON A LOW TRUNK

Pruning to create a low trunk is the best way of displaying trees grown for their attractive bark, such as Acer pensylvanicum. *Maples "bleed" sap so are pruned only when fully dormant in early winter.*

Prune to 20in (50cm) above ground level, just above 2 pairs of strong shoots. Tip prune these by 4in (10cm)

Cut back dead or damaged wood to healthy buds

Remove lower shoots from main stems to display attractive bark to the maximum

Remove inward-facing sideshoots from main stems to keep the center open

Remove low sideshoots

Prune weak shoots to a bud 2in (5cm) from main stem

YEAR 1, WINTER   YEAR 2, WINTER   YEAR 3, WINTER

CARING FOR YOUNG TREES

T HE EFFORTS THAT YOU PUT INTO the early training and pruning of young trees are likely to be repaid throughout the tree's life. Many of the pruning cuts made during the early years aim to avoid later potential problems, such as congestion or heavy, unsafe branches at maturity. If a tree is trained properly when young, it will need little regular maintenance pruning later, although all trees benefit from regular checks for dead, diseased, damaged, or unsafe wood.

STAKING

All but the smallest single-stemmed and young feathered trees need a stake for the first two years until a strong trunk and root system are established. The stake does *not* hold the tree up but helps it form a straight, vertical stem. Flexing in the wind positively helps strengthen the trunk; in most cases, a short stake and tie is preferable. The stake, whether straight or angled, is driven at least 2ft (60cm) into the ground before planting, and the roots are spread around it. Ties must be secure but not inflexible.

LOW, ANGLED STAKE
Useful in exposed sites and for container-grown trees, this stake leans at 45° into the prevailing wind. An angled stake avoids the rootball.

LOW, STRAIGHT STAKE
A stake that is less than one third of the tree's height permits stem strengthening by flexing. It is best for bare-root trees.

◀ TWO-STAKE SYSTEM
Ideal for most, but especially balled-and-burlapped or container-grown trees; stakes are sited without damaging the rootball.

▶ EXTENDING A STAKE
Here, a tall stake supports a weeping standard in training. As the leading shoot grows, it is extended to greater heights by means of a strong stake.

NOT SO TIGHT

• Use a spacer with the tree tie to avoid chafing the stem bark; abrasions of the bark may allow wood-rotting organisms to enter.
• Check ties regularly, and loosen as the stem girth increases. If too tight, ties cut into the bark or constrict the stem, eventually killing the tree.

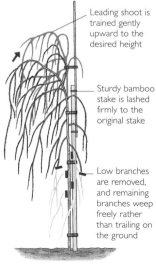

Leading shoot is trained gently upward to the desired height

Sturdy bamboo stake is lashed firmly to the original stake

Low branches are removed, and remaining branches weep freely rather than trailing on the ground

PROBLEMS WITH LEADERS

If a young tree develops two or more leading shoots, they compete with each other, so the desired form of the tree may be lost. At worst, the tree will develop two or more branches in the crown with a very narrow angle between them, which is likely to become structurally unsafe at maturity as the branches gain height and weight. This situation can lead to large branches breaking in high winds or ice storms. The damage may be irremediable and the tree lost altogether. It is especially important to remedy this with central-leader trees. The topmost shoot will not always be the best choice as the new leader; always select the strongest and most upright shoot.

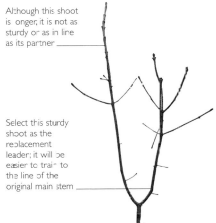

Although this shoot is longer, it is not as sturdy or as in line as its partner

Select this sturdy shoot as the replacement leader; it will be easier to train to the line of the original main stem

Although it is not the topmost one, this strong, upright shoot is the best candidate to become the new leader

COMPETING LEADERS
This young tree has developed several competing leading shoots in an upright cluster at the tree's apex. A single leader must be selected and the rest removed if the tree is to become a structurally strong mature specimen.

DUAL-LEADER PROBLEMS
On trees with opposite buds, the loss of the leading shoot results in a pair of new shoots. Select the shoot that grows nearest to the line of the main stem, then remove the other shoot, making a neat, clean cut at its base.

HOW TO REPAIR A BROKEN LEADER

If a leading shoot is broken by wind, damaged by cold, or dies back, prune it back to the nearest strong sideshoot that can be trained in to the vertical as its replacement. If there are no suitable sideshoots, prune it back to a strong bud and train in the new shoot that results as the replacement. Tie in the replacement shoot to a sturdy stake to train the shoot to the vertical. The stake can be removed once the new growth has become firm and woody.

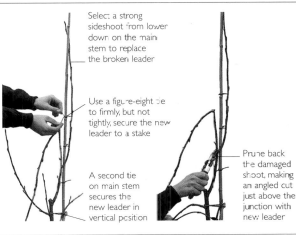

Select a strong sideshoot from lower down on the main stem to replace the broken leader

Use a figure-eight tie to firmly, but not tightly, secure the new leader to a stake

A second tie on main stem secures the new leader in vertical position

Prune back the damaged shoot, making an angled cut just above the junction with new leader

MAINTAINING ESTABLISHED TREES

IF PROPERLY TRAINED WHEN YOUNG, established trees seldom need regular pruning, although all trees benefit from regular health checks throughout their lives. For most, the best time to check for and correct defects is in late summer, or in midwinter when the branch framework is at its most visible. The removal of suckers and routine removal of dead, diseased, and damaged wood should be dealt with promptly, as soon as it is noticed.

CORRECTING UNEVEN GROWTH

Common causes of uneven growth are shade cast by buildings or other trees and exposure to wind. There is no point in pruning unless the cause is dealt with first. Remove the cause or provide shelter, then restore over several years, removing only one or two branches each year (*see p.11*). Prune weak branches hard in year one. In subsequent years, thin regrowth and shorten or remove other branches to restore the symmetry.

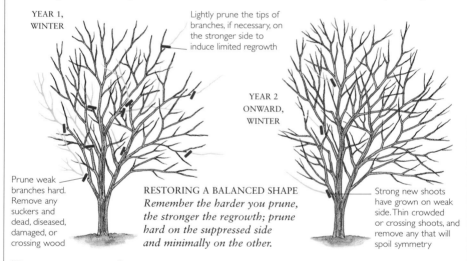

YEAR 1,
WINTER

Lightly prune the tips of branches, if necessary, on the stronger side to induce limited regrowth

YEAR 2
ONWARD,
WINTER

Prune weak branches hard. Remove any suckers and dead, diseased, damaged, or crossing wood

RESTORING A BALANCED SHAPE
Remember the harder you prune, the stronger the regrowth; prune hard on the suppressed side and minimally on the other.

Strong new shoots have grown on weak side. Thin crowded or crossing shoots, and remove any that will spoil symmetry

REMOVING SUCKERS

Suckers often arise from the roots or trunk of a tree in response to injury and may also occur from the rootstock of grafted plants, below the desirable grafted cultivar. They divert energy from the tree and can be a nuisance. They should be removed as seen.

BACK TO BASE
Whether on root or trunk, remove suckers at the point of origin. If you pull or dig up root suckers, dormant buds shoot into growth; trace to the base, pull off sharply, then trim wound with a sharp knife to remove dormant buds.

Cut off suckers at the point of origin; better still, rub out buds when still tiny

Root suckers may arise some distance from the tree

THINNING REGROWTH

Hard pruning often stimulates the growth of whippy, fast-growing shoots known as watersprouts. They arise from dormant buds beneath the bark near the site of the pruning wound. If all of these shoots are left in place, they divert energy from the rest of the tree, can cause overcrowding, and rarely make structurally strong branches. If they are carefully thinned, however, they can be transformed to strong replacement branches. Where a damaged branch has been clumsily lopped, careful thinning can also do much to improve the appearance of an awkward-looking stub.

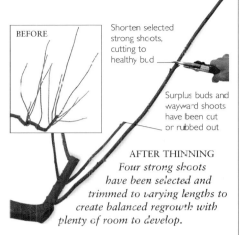

BEFORE

Shorten selected strong shoots, cutting to healthy bud

Surplus buds and wayward shoots have been cut or rubbed out

AFTER THINNING
Four strong shoots have been selected and trimmed to varying lengths to create balanced regrowth with plenty of room to develop.

MAJOR TREE SURGERY

Never attempt to remove any branches yourself that cannot be reached from the ground and whose weight you cannot safely support unaided. Major tree surgery is dangerous and should be done only by a professional arborist. If a tree does outgrow its space, or it produces branches that overhang a street or other property or obstruct power lines or utilities, crown lifting or reduction helps avoid needing to fell the tree. Always check with the local authority whether the tree has any legal protection before any work is done. Such operations are seldom necessary if you chose the right tree for the site, so always check the mature dimensions before planting.

Lower branches are removed to create a longer length of clear trunk

CROWN LIFTING
Used to removed branches that obstruct free passage or visibility, block out light, or obscure street signs or lighting. It is also useful if you wish to plant beneath the tree.

Branches are removed from the center and shortened at the extremities

CROWN THINNING AND REDUCTION
Used to reduce the overall height and spread of a canopy and to relieve congestion in and reduce wind resistance of the crown; it may also be done to permit passage of power lines.

COPPICING AND POLLARDING

THE TRADITIONAL WOODLAND MANAGEMENT techniques of coppicing and pollarding consist of hard pruning on a regular basis. In gardens, they can be used to produce vigorous, brilliantly colored young stems or larger than normal, more ornamental leaves. Not all plants respond well; they must be tough and have the ability to resist disease to enable them to recover from such regular wounding. Fertilize and mulch after such drastic pruning.

POLLARDING

Pollards are created by cutting stems back to a clear length of trunk at some height above the ground. Willows and dogwoods are often treated in this way to give a display of brilliantly colored winter stems that contrast with other plantings. It is also a good way to produce more colorful or more ornamental leaves that can be appreciated at eye level. Stems are cut back each or every second or third year in spring, just before or as growth begins, to secure the longest possible bark display.

Pollarding is sometimes done to large trees, such as sycamores (*Platanus*), in street situations. Such skilled, dangerous work should be done only by arborists.

DEVELOPING A POLLARD
Once a young tree develops a head of branches on a clear stem of the desired height, saw through the stem just above a sizable cluster of branches.

ESTABLISHED POLLARD
Every 1–3 years, cut back all stems in late winter or early spring to within ¾in (2cm) of the main stem. Thin new shoots to avoid overcrowding.

WINTER STEMS
Colorful stems on a clear trunk of 5ft (1.5m) give a winter and spring display that forms a canopy well above other border plants.

TREES AND SHRUBS FOR COPPICING AND POLLARDING

Acer negundo 'Flamingo' for larger, colorful leaves.

Catalpa bignonioides 'Aurea' for larger, colorful leaves.

Cornus alba, C. sanguinea and cultivars for winter stems.

Corylus avellana 'Aurea', *C. maxima* 'Purpurea' for larger, colorful leaves.

Cotinus coggygria for larger, more colorful leaves.

Eucalyptus gunnii for colorful juvenile leaves.

Paulownia tomentosa for exceptionally large leaves.

Rubus cockburnianus , R. thibetanus for white winter stems.

Sambucus nigra, S. racemosa and colored and cut-leaved cultivars for larger and more colorful leaves.

Salix alba, S. daphnoides and cultivars for very colorful winter stems.

Vitex agnus-castus for large clusters of flowers.

PRUNING FOR ENHANCED FOLIAGE

All trees and shrubs that tolerate hard pruning produce larger, more colorful leaves if pruned hard, because the plant's energy is directed into lush new growth. *Eucalyptus* produce both juvenile and adult leaves; the juveniles on new growth are usually more highly colored. In trees or shrubs that flower on older wood, enhanced foliage is gained at the expense of flowers.

◄ AFTER PRUNING
Here, on Eucalyptus gunnii, *growth is cut back to a low pollard each or every other year in spring.*

► FRESH FOLIAGE
The strong new growth bears round, juvenile leaves of silvery blue-gray.

COPPICING

Coppicing is very similar to pollarding except that the regular (sometimes annual) pruning is taken back to ground level at the end of the dormant season. As with pollarding, the tree or shrub has a full-sized root system, so the regrowth is well fed,

exceptionally vigorous, and often shows more intense color. Cutting back to low levels is also useful for marginally hardy plants such as *Eucalyptus*, since it makes it practical to provide the winter protection of a mulch over the entire plant.

WASTE NOT...

• Cut sections of willow stems root easily; they take root even if pushed directly into the ground. One way to exploit this ability is to make living, woven-willow fences or hedges; they make ideal screens or windbreaks.

• The cut stems of willows and hazels can be woven or tied together to make useful items for the garden, such as low fences for border edging, tripods and other plant supports, rustic trellises, and bird nesting sites.

AFTER PRUNING
All growth has been cut back almost to ground level in winter. Do not cut below the soil surface or injure the swollen, woody base from which new shoots develop.

REGROWTH
The new shoots arise from the outer edges of the coppiced stems. If they are too dense, they can be thinned by cutting them out at the base, rather than shortening them.

CARING FOR CONIFERS

MOST CONIFERS ARE CONE-BEARING evergreen trees with scale- or needle-like leaves and, with a few exceptions, are grown with minimal pruning at both juvenile and adult stages. Nearly all have upright growth with strongly dominant leading shoots and so will readily produce a conical shape, providing the leader remains undamaged. Once mature, pruning is best avoided altogether, unless to repair damage or remove reverted or wayward growth.

SINGLING OUT A LEADER

Occasionally, usually as a result of damage to the leading bud, conifers produce dual leaders. It is vital to remove one of them to produce a well-shaped specimen and to avoid potentially dangerous narrow branch forks at maturity. Most conifers "bleed" profusely when cut; prune in autumn or winter to keep bleeding to a minimum.

Select the straightest shoot as the new leader, and cut off the crooked one at its base

COMPETING LEADERS
To maintain the single-stemmed, conical habit if two leading shoots occur, it is essential to cut out the weaker or more crooked shoot cleanly at its base.

REPLACING A BROKEN LEADER

Most conifers will naturally form a new leading shoot if damage occurs when the tree is still young. If damage occurs, often a result of wind or snow-load injury, select and train in a new leader as soon as possible. If there is no obvious new leading shoot, select a strong sideshoot from lower down and tie it in vertically. Even if it was growing nearly horizontally, it will soon assume the role of dominant leader.

1 A damaged leader can be replaced by a strong sideshoot that can be trained to assume the dominant role.

2 Remove all damaged growth, cutting back cleanly to a strong, preferably upright shoot lower down.

3 Insert a stake at the tree's center, then tie in new leader. Once the leader grows strongly upward, remove the stake.

SPLAYED SHOOTS

Conifers are susceptible to damage by winds, ice, or a heavy fall of snow, which can cause branches to splay out and spoil the form of the tree. (Always remove lying snow to minimize the risk.) If a branch does splay out, trace it back to its point of origin and check that it has not split from the trunk. If it has, remove it and deal with the gap as shown below. If it is undamaged, tie it back in to the main shoot (*right*).

TYING IN SPLAYED-OUT GROWTH
Use soft materials, such as tarred twine, rubber tree ties, or nylon stockings, to tie undamaged shoots back in to the main shoot or trunk as you ease it back gently into place.

Branch splayed out under the weight of snow

DEALING WITH DEAD PATCHES

Very few conifers have the ability to regrow from old wood, and scorched or dead foliage must be cut out completely. Unless the damage is very slight, this often leaves an unsightly hole, especially in formally shaped trees or hedges (*see pp.50–53*).

Slight damage can be disguised by tying adjacent shoots across the gap, as for splayed-out growth (*above*). In more severe cases, this may not be possible, so secure a stake to a main shoot or branch, then tie neighboring shoots to that instead.

1 **Remove all dead**, scorched, or damaged shoots completely, cutting them back cleanly to a main stem or branch. The gap reveals old, internal branches (with sparse, if any foliage) that are seldom able to resprout.

2 **Secure a stake** to a main stem or branch. Draw healthy neighboring branches across the gap and tie them in. New growth that arises from the young wood will soon disguise the stake.

ORNAMENTAL SHRUBS

THE AIMS OF PRUNING

WITH THEIR PERMANENT WOODY framework, shrubs bring an enduring presence to a planting. Many are chosen for their beautiful foliage and may need only minimal pruning, but those that bear flowers or fruit usually need regular pruning if they are to perform their best. With these, the aim of pruning is to remove older, unproductive wood in favor of young, healthy, vigorous growth that nearly always flowers more abundantly.

GOOD REASONS TO PRUNE

Unless they are to be trained for special effects (such as topiary , most shrubs look best when allowed to assume their natural habit and size. It is important to choose the shrub to fit the space, rather than to prune constantly to restrict growth, which may reduce its ornamental potential. To stay vigorous and handsome, many shrubs need only light pruning to shape. with routine removal of dead, diseased, or damaged growth. In those that need regular pruning to enhance flowering, correct pruning at the right time is essential: critical factors are the age of flowering wood and time of flowering. Before making any pruning cuts, you should have a clear aim in mind of the results you intend and expect.

BUDDLEJA 'LOCHINCH' Correct pruning ensures a neat, rounded form, the best possible foliage, and an abundance of late summer flowers that look beautiful and attract butterflies.

◀ HYDRANGEA PANICULATA 'FLORIBUNDA' *flowers in late summer on the current season's wood.*

BUYING GOOD SHRUBS

Y OUNG SHRUBS THAT YOU BUY AS container-grown specimens in the garden center or nursery will probably already be a few years old, and most may have undergone some initial pruning and training to shape. You may also choose to propagate your own from seed, cuttings, or layers, which gives you control over the growing conditions and the opportunity to train your own well-shaped specimen from scratch.

CHOOSING GOOD SPECIMENS

Young plants should be vigorous and healthy, with a well-balanced framework of strong stems clothed in undamaged, pest- and disease-free leaves of good color. If plants are grafted, check that the graft union (a slight swelling where graft meets rootstock) is a smooth, straight join, without prominent kinks in the stem. Check that the root system fills, but is not crowded in, the pot and that it does not protrude from the bottom.

WHAT TO LOOK FOR
• Look for a good balance of top-growth to root growth; a plant in too small a pot may be rootbound and may not establish well.
• Avoid buying plants that have been encouraged to flower heavily to promote sale. If you do obtain such a plant, try to deadhead and fertilize it as soon as possible.
• Avoid buying plants with obvious signs of pests and diseases or disorders caused by poor nutrition, such as leaf yellowing.

Healthy shoot tips with no sign of scorch or dieback

Older leaves are glossy and healthy

Young foliage is abundant, healthy and glossy

With insufficient nutrients to sustain the foliage, stems have become bare and leggy

Top-growth is far too extensive in comparison with the volume of roots

Dead growth begins to crowd the plant center

Roots are crowded in the pot

GOOD CHOICE
A pot of ample size filled with healthy roots sustains a well-balanced framework of sturdy, evenly spaced stems showing lots of new growth. The leaves of this camellia are glossy and plentiful, and both younger and older leaves are of a rich healthy color.

POOR CHOICE
A congested rootball suggests the plant has been in its pot for too long, and a compacted root system will not establish well. The soil mix has been exhausted of nutrients and is unable to sustain new top-growth: the existing top-growth has begun to die back.

Unbalanced Specimens

An unbalanced root-to-shoot ratio – where top-growth is too extensive for the rootball to sustain – is a primary cause of poor growth after planting. Unless remedial action is taken, a container-grown plant that has outgrown its pot will seldom establish well. The top-growth can be pruned back by up to half its length, which will ensure strong, bushy growth later. Alternatively, some of the stems can be cut back hard almost to the base, which will encourage, taller straighter stems.

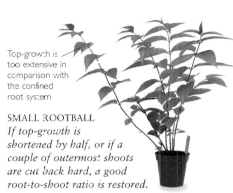

Top-growth is too extensive in comparison with the confined root system

SMALL ROOTBALL
If top-growth is shortened by half, or if a couple of outermost shoots are cut back hard, a good root-to-shoot ratio is restored.

Pruning upon Planting

A well-chosen plant needs little pruning upon planting, other than perhaps to prune the tips of soft growth to encourage bushiness, or to reduce overly long shoots by a third of their length to promote a more balanced outline. It is routine to remove weak growth as well as damaged shoots and shoot tips. If plants have flowered, deadhead them so that the plant uses energy for growth rather than seed production. Check for and trim away any roots that have been damaged, and tease out any roots that have been coiled around in the pot. If young plants have been grown from cuttings, additional pruning to induce a bushy habit may be necessary.

Growing tip is cut back to a strong bud

The cutting branches just below the point to which it was pruned

EVERGREEN SHRUBS
Cuttings of evergreens, such as ceanothus, are more likely to branch naturally in their first year and seldom need additional pruning to promote bushiness.

Strong, straight stem produces upward growth

Low branches occur naturally low down on the stem, leading to a neat, balanced, and (in this case) conical shape

DECIDUOUS SHRUBS
The growing tip of a young, single-stemmed forsythia is cut back to a strong bud to induce branching. Two sideshoots develop, laying a foundation for a bushier habit at maturity.

ROUTINE TASKS

C HECK OVER YOUR SHRUBS REGULARLY to remove any dead or diseased growth promptly before it becomes a problem. Make deadheading and the removal of unwanted growth, such as suckers or reverted shoots, part of your routine. Most important, keep the soil around shrubs weed free, and apply fertilizer in spring to promote strong growth. Use a mulch to reduce the need to weed and to help retain soil moisture throughout the growing season.

REMOVING SUCKERS

There are several types of suckers. Some are desirable, such as those that grow naturally to increase a shrub's spread. Whippy shoots that grow in inappropriate places, often in response to damage, and those that appear from below the graft union in grafted plants are undesirable and must be removed.

Leaves are smaller, unevenly margined, and a paler green than on the desirable cultivar's shoots

DESIRABLE GROWTH

IDENTIFYING SUCKERS
The leaf shape of a sucker usually differs from that of the desirable grafted cultivar (here a Hamamelis*).*

SUCKER

REMOVING SUCKERS
Trace the sucker back to its point of origin on the stem or on the root, and pull it sharply away. Use a sharp knife to neaten the wound without enlarging it, cleanly paring off any remaining tissue. This also removes any dormant buds that may sprout later.

DEADHEADING AFTER FLOWERING

The function of flowers is to produce seed to sustain the species. It takes considerable energy to produce seed, and it is often preferable that this energy is diverted into new growth. In most cases, spent flowers are removed with pruners, but in some shrubs, such as rhododendrons, vulnerable new growth buds lie beneath the spent flowers, so pinching with your finger and thumb is a safer option.

PINCHING OUT
Trace back the flower stalk to its base, and look out for the new growth buds. Pinch out the dead flower(s), taking care not to damage the new growth buds.

NEW GROWTH BUD
A new bud (just below and to one side of the old flower stalk) has already started into growth. It is very vulnerable to damage at this stage.

DEADHEADING FLOWER CLUSTERS

Although deadheading is not strictly
essential, and shrubs will bloom in subsequent years even if it s not done, it does
prevent unwanted self-seeding. The energy
it conserves usually improves growth in the
current season as well as flowering the
following year. In some cases, as with
Buddleja, it may result in a second crop
of flowers in the same season. The sooner
it is done after the flowers have faded, the
better. Single flowers can simply be nipped
off along with their stalk. With shrubs that
produce clusters of flowers, the entire
flowerhead is cut back to buds or young
sideshoots lower down on the plant.

CUTTING OUT
*Cut back flowered
shoots to healthy
buds or young
sideshoots, removing
the entire flower
cluster with pruners.*

On *Buddleja*, the
lower sideshoots
often produce
smaller flower
clusters at their tips,
giving a second,
smaller display

CUTTING OUT REVERTED GROWTH

Sometimes, plants produce unusual growth
of a different color or form to that of the
species. Known as a sport or mutation,
such growth is often very ornamental, and
the sport may be propagated to produce
very desirable plants. Many dwarf conifers
are the products of reverted growth.

If the sport returns to its original form, this
is referred to as reversion. Variegated
plants, for example, occasionally produce
shoots with plain green foliage. Reverted
shoots are usually more vigorous than their
ornamental counterpart and, if not removed,
may eventually dominate the plant.

WHY REMOVE REVERSIONS?
• Variegated leaves contain less chlorophyll
(essential for energy production) than plain
green ones. The shoots grow less strongly and
are easily outcompeted by the green growth.
• When dwarf conifers revert, the growth is
likely to be stronger and of a different shape
or habit, which spoils the form.

Cut back reverted shoot
at its point of origin; the
cut will be masked by
the remaining foliage

▲ VARIEGATED SHRUBS
*Cut out all-green shoots on variegated plants
as soon as noticed, removing them entirely at
their point of origin.*

◀ MAINTAINING SHAPE IN DWARF CONIFERS
*Reverted shoots commonly grow strongly
upward, outward, or in some other atypical
direction and should be removed.*

PRUNING SHRUBS

THROUGHOUT THEIR LIVES, shrubs need the routine removal of dead, diseased, and damaged wood. Once they have had a growing season in which to establish and have become dormant, begin to establish a framework of well-balanced branches to display their ornamental features at their best. Thereafter, pruning to enhance performance varies; some, like *Daphne* and *Hamamelis*, need little or no pruning, while others perform best with an annual program.

FORMATIVE PRUNING

Most deciduous shrubs require formative pruning to some degree. The aim is to create an open-centered framework that allows free passage of light and air to sustain strong, healthy growth throughout the shrub. Shrubs that flower on the current season's growth (after midsummer) will usually be pruned back to the framework each spring, so it is important to create a foundation of strong stems from the outset. With spring-flowering shrubs, which flower on older wood, an open-centered framework is even more important. Remove crossing or crowded stems, cutting them back to a bud that faces in an outward direction. Evergreen shrubs usually develop a neat habit naturally, so little formative pruning is needed. If necessary, remove cold-damaged or weak stems, and prune the tips of overly long growth to balance the outline.

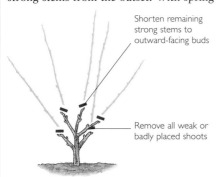

Shorten remaining strong stems to outward-facing buds

Remove all weak or badly placed shoots

A FIRM FOUNDATION

• When creating a low framework for shrubs that flower on the current season's growth, imagine the initial shape as an open hand, palm upward, with branches spaced evenly around the palm.

• Because shrubs that flower on older wood will retain a greater proportion of their wood from year to year, they are more likely to develop a tangle of branches at their centers unless well-trained when young.

▲ A LOW FRAMEWORK
A framework of strong stems is a perfect foundation for shrubs flowering on the current season's growth; it will be extended as the shrub grows.

▶ CREATE AN OPEN CENTER
Early pruning ensures a well-shaped shrub that has an uncluttered center at maturity. Remove unwanted stems when they are still small and the plant is young; their wounds will heal rapidly.

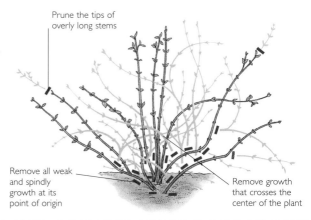

Prune the tips of overly long stems

Remove all weak and spindly growth at its point of origin

Remove growth that crosses the center of the plant

PRUNING ESTABLISHED EARLY-FLOWERING SHRUBS

The timing of pruning to enhance flowering in all established shrubs is crucial. If you prune at the wrong time, you may remove most of the shoots that bear the coming season's flowers. Shrubs that flower early in the season, between late winter and midsummer, bloom on wood made in the previous growing season. Pruning directly after flowering each year allows them to produce a new crop of strong shoots during the growing season that will bear flowers the following year.

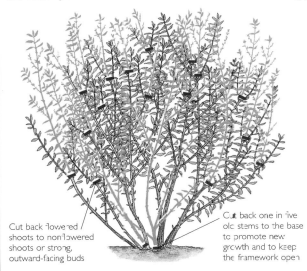

Cut back flowered shoots to nonflowered shoots or strong, outward-facing buds

Cut back one in five old stems to the base to promote new growth and to keep the framework open

GOOD EXAMPLES

Deutzia flowers from mid-spring to midsummer.
Forsythia blooms between late winter and midspring.
Lonicera fragrantissima: late winter and early spring.
Philadelphus: early- to midsummer-flowering.
Spiraea 'Arguta' blooms in spring.

CONSTANT RENEWAL
Removing the old shoots, which flower less freely with age, encourages replacement with more vigorous, freely flowering young ones.

PRUNING CANE-FORMING SHRUBS

Some shrubs produce their new growth as canelike shoots that arise from the base of the plant. The canes themselves often give a very elegant habit. In this case, shortening flowered shoots would lead to an ungainly, top-heavy bush, so flowered canes are cut back to the base or to strong buds or sideshoots near the base. If they flower early, prune after flowering; if they flower after midsummer, prune in early spring.

GOOD EXAMPLES

Cytisus scoparius and hybrids Prune annually after flowering in late spring, from an early age. They will not regrow from old wood.
Leycesteria formosa Flowers in late summer; prune in early spring.
Euphorbia characias Prune after flowering in midsummer; leave all unflowered shoots in place. Avoid contact with the irritant sap.

Cut about one in three flowered shoots back to the base to promote strong new shoots

PRUNING KERRIA JAPONICA
Prune after flowering in spring; the new, pea-green canes that result become part of the appeal that carries into winter.

PRUNING LATE-FLOWERING DECIDUOUS SHRUBS

Late-flowering deciduous shrubs – those that flower between midsummer and late autumn – bear their flowers on new shoots made in the current growing season. They are pruned each year in spring as the new buds begin to swell. The previous year's flowered stems are cut back to a permanent woody framework. This is formed in the early years (*see p.40*) and is usually allowed to develop to slightly higher levels above ground as the shrub matures. You can also vary the heights of the framework of this group of shrubs to gain graduated effects in a large shrub border. The technique is especially useful with shrubs that are vigorous but may be marginally hardy, such as *Phygelius* and *Clerodendrum bungei*, since all of the winter-damaged growth is cut back; with these, it is best to delay pruning until danger of frost has passed.

◀ PRUNING *BUDDLEJA DAVIDII*
In spring, as the buds begin to burst into growth, all of the previous year's stems are cut back to within two to three pairs of healthy buds of the woody framework. You may need to use loppers to thin out the older framework stems.

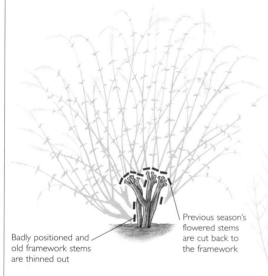

Badly positioned and old framework stems are thinned out

Previous season's flowered stems are cut back to the framework

GOOD CANDIDATES

Buddleja crispa, B. davidii cultivars, **B. fallowiana, B. 'Lochinch', B. × weyeriana** and other late-flowering buddlejas.

Caryopteris × clandonensis and cultivars, with clusters of blue flowers in late summer-autumn.

Clerodendrum bungei, deep pink flowers; late summer to autumn.

Indigofera amblyantha, I. heterantha, spires of pealike flowers from summer to autumn.

Phygelius aequalis, P. capensis, P × rectus, and cultivars, with spires of tubular yellow, orange, pink, or red flowers from midsummer into autumn.

Each year, in spring, cut all flowered stems back to within three or four buds of the old wood. Varying the height of cut gives a more graceful, natural-looking plant

Cut out any sections of the framework that produced no flowers last year

▲ PRUNING A PEROVSKIA
If pruned regularly, Perovskia will produce vigorous flowering shoots from a basal framework for many years.

◀ PRUNING OLD FRAMEWORK
As the plant ages, the framework becomes congested and the oldest sections cease to produce shoots; they should be removed in spring.

PRUNING LAVENDERS AND HEATHERS

This group also includes other low-growing, shrubby evergreens that flower in spring, or from mid- to late summer on. They are treated the same way, but winter or spring-bloomers – such as some of the heathers – are pruned after flowering, and later-flowerers, for example lavender, are pruned in spring. The group includes several gray-leaved Mediterranean plants that are valued for their foliage and flowers. In hot, dry climates, they can be pruned hard right after flowering. Many are not reliably hardy in cold, wet winters. Here, it is safer to restrict autumn pruning to deadheading, then complete pruning in spring after danger of frost has passed.

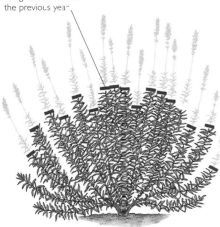

The flowered shoots are cut back to within a few buds of the growth made in the previous year

SUITABLE CANDIDATES

Artemisia abrotanum, A. 'Powis Castle' can be pruned as for lavender.
Calluna vulgaris cultivars are pruned in spring.
Erica carnea, E. × darleyensis and cultivars are pruned in spring as the last flowers fade; *E. cinerea* is trimmed lightly in early spring.
Helichrysum italicum is pruned as for lavender.
Santolina, lavender cotton, is pruned in the same way as lavender.

◀ PRUNING SHRUBBY EVERGREENS
Cut back all of this year's shoots to within ½–1in (1.5–2.5cm) of the previous year's growth; in spring for late-flowering plants, or after flowering for early-flowering plants. Where winters are cold and wet, prune slightly tender evergreens as for lavender (below).

AUTUMN DEADHEADING
In cold-winter climates, deadhead in autumn to neaten the plant and harvest the last of the flowers. Remaining top-growth gives some winter protection for buds lower on the stems.

SPRING PRUNING
When all danger of hard frost has passed, complete the pruning by cutting the remaining stems back hard. This can also be done effectively and quickly with hand shears.

PRUNING HYDRANGEAS

The most popular hydrangeas, *Hydrangea macrophylla* cultivars, bear flowers at the stem tips in mid- to late summer, but on the previous season's growth. Flowers come in two types: lacecaps, with large sterile flowers around a central cluster of small fertile flowers, and the mopheads or hortensias, with round heads of mainly sterile flowers. Nearly all flower well if left unpruned but produce a better display if pruned correctly. They need little formative pruning. Once established, cut back one or two of the old shoots to the base each year to promote new growth. Cut flowered shoots back to the fat buds on old wood that will produce the next season's flowers.

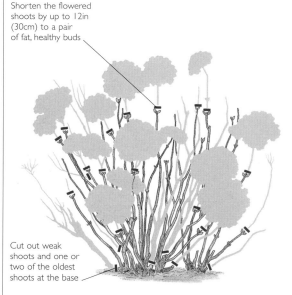

Shorten the flowered shoots by up to 12in (30cm) to a pair of fat, healthy buds

Cut out weak shoots and one or two of the oldest shoots at the base

WHEN TO PRUNE
• In milder areas, macrophylla hydrangeas can usually be pruned safely right after flowering.
• In colder, exposed areas, pruning is best delayed until midspring. This is so that growth killed by winter cold can be plainly differentiated from undamaged wood.

HYDRANGEA MACROPHYLLA These hydrangeas are long-lived and tolerate very hard pruning. Neglected bushes can be cut right back to ground level in spring to rejuvenate them, although they will not produce flowers until the following year.

HOW TO PRUNE *HYDRANGEA PANICULATA*

Hydrangea paniculata and its cultivars bear conical heads of flowers on the current year's growth in late summer. They flower well if left unpruned, but the flowerheads are much larger and more dramatic if plants are cut back to a framework each spring, just before they start into growth. After planting, create a framework of four or five main stems (*see p.40*). The framework can be as low as 10in (25cm), or 24in (60cm) or more, to provide height at the back of a border.

CREATING A FRAMEWORK
Each spring, cut all of the previous year's growth back to pairs of healthy buds as near as possible to the permanent woody framework.

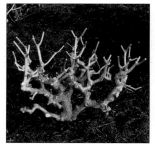

AFTER PRUNING
A low framework with plenty of room between the branches is the aim. Hydrangeas have opposite buds; each cut will result in two flowering shoots.

PRUNING EVERGREEN SHRUBS

Most evergreens need little pruning other than the routine removal of weak, dead, and diseased growth; the shortening of wayward branches, when necessary; and deadheading, unless they bear ornamental fruits. Evergreens do, however, often sustain winter damage from cold temperatures, heavy snow loads, or cold, dry winds. The removal of winter-damaged

growth should be delayed until the danger of all hard frost has passed. Cut back damaged shoots to healthy young shoots or to buds on undamaged wood.

The timing of routine pruning for evergreens is after flowering for those that flower between late winter and early spring, and in midspring for those that flower later in the season.

Shorten overly long or winter-damaged shoots, cutting back to a strong, healthy bud

Deadhead flowered stems where practical, taking care not to damage any growth buds that may be beneath the flowers

MINIMALLY PRUNED EVERGREENS
For evergreens such as camellias, gaultherias, and rhododendrons, just trim any shoots that are overly long or that spoil the outline in midspring. Deadhead, unless fruits are desired. (For deadheading rhododendrons, see p.38)

PRUNING ESTABLISHED EVERGREENS

In midspring, prune out straggly growth and diseased, damaged, or dead wood, using pruners or loppers. New growth will soon disguise the pruning cuts. Remove shoots to thin out congested or badly placed stems; reducing dense growth is especially important in areas of heavy snowfall. Deadhead, unless fruits are needed, cutting back to a healthy nonflowered sideshoot.

GOOD EXAMPLES

Aucuba japonica and cultivars in midspring.
Carpenteria californica after flowering.
Eucryphia × nymansensis and cultivars in mid- to late spring.
Pieris japonica and cultivars after flowering.
Pittosporum tenuifolium in midspring.
Prunus lusitanica in late spring.

ESTABLISHED EVERGREENS
Although the majority of evergreens need only light pruning, some, such as Aucuba, Berberis julianae, and Prunus laurocerasus, tolerate hard pruning when they need renovating.

RENOVATING SHRUBS

WHEN YOU TAKE OVER A NEW GARDEN, or as an established garden matures, you are often confronted with neglected and overgrown shrubs. If they are basically healthy and tolerate hard pruning, many can be rejuvenated by cutting back hard. Those that are short lived or don't respond well to hard pruning as they age, such as *Santolina* and lavenders, are best replaced. It's also easier to replace common, fast-growing shrubs such as flowering currants (*Ribes*).

REJUVENATING A NEGLECTED SHRUB

Deciduous shrubs are best renovated while they are dormant (between autumn and early spring), and evergreens as they come into growth in midspring. You may lose a season's flowers, but the compensation is a reinvigorated specimen that will flower for many years to come. Renovation can also be done at the normal pruning time for the particular shrub; early-flowering shrubs, such as *Philadelphus*, can be pruned hard immediately after flowering, with no loss of the following season's flowers. If there's any doubt that the shrub will respond well to drastic pruning, renovate in two or three stages. Always fertilize and mulch well after pruning to encourage strong new growth.

RENOVATING A *PHILADELPHUS*
You can cut the entire shrub back to ground level, but for the sake of retaining a presence in the border, in the first year, remove up to half of the oldest stems at ground level, concentrating on removing crossing and rubbing stems and dead, diseased, and damaged wood.

CUT YOUR LOSSES
It is not worth renovating sickly plants, and if a diseased shrub can't be treated to restore health, it is best replaced. Plants that tolerate hard pruning in their prime may not respond when old. Propagate favorite plants to replace them.

Shorten to a bud any sideshoots from main stems that grow across the center of the shrub

Shorten the remaining healthy shoots by half their length, cutting to a bud or vigorous sideshoot, aiming to produce an open center

Cut out dead, diseased, and damaged stems at the base. Cut crossing and rubbing stems, and up to half of the oldest stems, to within 2–3in (5–8cm) of ground level

REMOVE STEMS
Use pruners to remove more slender stems at the base. For larger, thicker stems, you may need to use a pruning saw or loppers. Take care to avoid damaging the remaining stems.

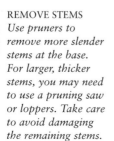

SHORTEN STEMS
Cut back healthy stems to a vigorous young sideshoot or healthy bud. On most shrubs, younger wood is of a paler color, and the bark usually smoother than that of old wood.

STAGED RENOVATION

Large shrubs, and those in which there is doubt of their response to drastic renovation, are best renovated over two or three years. Many evergreens, in particular, may die of shock or make only weak growth if all the foliage is removed at once, but they often respond extremely well to staged renovation. After removing all the dead wood, target the oldest and least productive branches in the first year.

NEGLECTED RHODODENDRON
In year one, in midspring, remove all the dead, diseased, and damaged wood. Then take out up to one third of the oldest and least productive main stems. You may need to thin the resulting new shoots to produce a well-balanced framework by cutting them back lightly.

Use a pruning saw to cut old stems back to the ground level. Many shrubs, including rhododendrons, are grafted; in which case, cut back to just above the graft union

In years two and three remove half of the remaining old stems so that at completion, all the old wood has been replaced with new

DRASTIC RENOVATION

A number of deciduous shrubs, such as lilacs (*Syringa*), tolerate the most drastic of pruning, and these can be renovated in one fell swoop when dormant. The strongest stems are then selected from the regrowth, and the rest are thinned out. If they are left in place, you will end up with a badly overcrowded shrub that seldom looks graceful and that also may be more susceptible to disease.

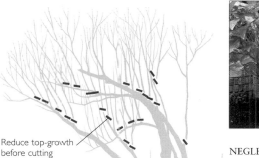

Reduce top-growth before cutting back main stems

Cut main stems back to a low framework 1–2ft (30–60cm) above ground; this avoids the graft union

REGROWTH
Regrowth will be vigorous, with lots of new shoots emerging from the stumps. In the next dormant season, reduce them to two or three evenly placed, strong shoots per stump.

NEGLECTED LILAC
If the plant is grafted (and cultivars usually are), do not cut below the graft union. Remove all of the suckers at the base; they will be from the rootstock. The heaviest branches are best shortened first before cutting to the base.

CREATING TOPIARY SHAPES

TOPIARY IS A FORM OF LIVING SCULPTURE created by the close clipping of mainly evergreen plants. Traditionally, a variety of geometric shapes, such as cones, spirals, and obelisks, were created to decorate formal gardens. They are perfect for flanking an entrance, big or small, or for framing a view. The more whimsical forms – birds, animals, even lettering – that are more difficult but fun to create have also long been used for more informal effects.

SHAPES AND EFFECTS

Plants used for topiary must have a dense habit, produce pliable growth, and tolerate regular close clipping. If a fine-textured surface and crisp outline is required, they should also have small leaves, like those of the traditional favorite, boxwood (*Buxus sempervirens*). It is also very important that the species used should be totally hardy in your climate and soil conditions; dieback and scorching rapidly spoils a neat and form, and the damage is difficult to remedy. Simple shapes are easily created by clipping alone; more complex forms are usually trained on wire frames.

SPECIAL EFFECTS
Simple, eye-catching forms are created by combining simple pruning and training. They need precise annual or twice-yearly clipping and regular maintenance.

A sweet bay standard (*Laurus nobilis*) trained with a clear stem and close-clipped head

Clipped from a bushy shrub with a fixed-length guide-line used as a compass from the stem

A simple shape to clip, especially in juniper, boxwood, yew, or cypress

STANDARD THREE-TIER BASIC CONE

PLANTS SUITABLE FOR TOPIARY

Artemisia abrotanum
(for short-lived specimens)
Berberis
Boxwood (*Buxus microphylla,
B. sempervirens*, and their
cultivars)
Hawthorn (*Crataegus*)
Cupressus sempervirens
Elaeagnus angustifolia

Euonymus fortunei
Ficus benjamina
Holly (*Ilex aquifolium,
I. crenata*, and others)
Juniper (*Juniperus*)
Laurus nobilis
Privet (*Ligustrum*)
Lonicera nitida
Myrtle (*Myrtus communis*)

Osmanthus
Phillyrea
Portugal laurel (*Prunus
lusitanica*)
Lavender cotton (*Santolina
chamaecyparissus*)
Wall germander, *Teucrium
chamaedrys* (short-lived)
Yew (*Taxus baccata*)

CLIPPING TO CREATE SHAPES

When clipping so closely and precisely, it is imperative that tools are kept sharp at all times. Take your time when clipping, and stand back often to check for discrepancies. Do not cut too much in one place at any one time; rather, work over the entire shape a little at a time. You are then less likely to make a mistake that may take several seasons to correct. Work from the top downward, and from the center outward, moving from side to side to maintain balance and symmetry. Even if you have a good eye, you will get the best results using straight edges as a guide.

1 **In the first year,** this bushy young boxwood (*Buxus*) is clipped roughly to shape using pruners. This will encourage the desirable and necessary dense, bushy growth.

2 **In the second year,** using a tripod of stakes and wire hoops as a guide, the bush is clipped to form a precise cone with a crisp and densely textured surface.

3 **In year three** and in subsequent years, the finished plant is clipped two or three times a year, depending on growth rate, to retain the sharp outline.

STANDARDS

A standard like this sweet bay (*Laurus nobilis*) is expensive to buy but easy to create. Prune a young, straight-stemmed plant back to a cluster of sideshoots at the top, shortening these to outward-facing buds. Clear all shoots from the stem. In subsequent years, keep the stem clear by rubbing out any buds as they appear. As new shoots appear on the crown, prune their tips to maintain a dense head.

CARING FOR A STANDARD SWEET BAY
Where not hardy, bring the plant under cover for the winter months. Fertilize each spring as growth begins, and keep watered during the growing season. Dust can be removed from the leaves with a fine spray from a hose.

Clear the stem of shoots and buds

Shorten the shoots at the crown to outward-facing buds in spring

Remove suckers from the base

YEAR 1

YEAR 2

LOOKING AFTER HEDGES

HEDGES MAKE A SUPERB BACKDROP to other plantings in the garden, can provide security and privacy, filter strong winds and dust, and act as a buffer to noise from nearby roads. With the right choice of species, they also provide food and a valuable haven for nesting birds. You can chose hedge plants for a formal style, which will be clipped closely and regularly, or for more informal situations, which need less regular shearing.

FORMATIVE PRUNING

The early pruning of a hedge ensures that it is well clothed to the base, with a dense network of branches at maturity. Prepare a band of ground, 3ft (1m) wide, then plant 1–2ft (30–60cm) apart in a straight line. Shorten leading shoots and sideshoots by a third of their length, and weak ones by two-thirds. Cut vigorous plants, such as hawthorn, to 6–12in (15–30cm). Do not cut conifers until they reach the desired height.

Leading shoot and strong sideshoots are shortened by a third of their length

Shorten weak shoots by two-thirds

A BRANCHING HABIT
Early pruning aims to create a dense branch system with plenty of sideshoots low down on the plant.

TRIMMING AND CUTTING METHODS

The tools that you use are determined by the size of the hedge. A large hedge demands the use of power trimmers; it would be time-consuming to use hand shears, even though you can achieve a finer surface (and make fewer mistakes) with them. Hedges of large-leaved plants are cut with pruners; other methods shred the leaves and leave jagged edges. Keep trimming tools sharp, clean, and well-oiled. Use a circuit breaker with power tools, and never use them in damp or wet conditions. Don't over-reach yourself; use scaffolding for hedges over head height, or consider using contractors.

HAND SHEARS
Keep the blades of shears parallel with the line of the hedge, so that the top and sides are cut evenly and flat and you do not inadvertently gouge holes in the surface.

HEDGE TRIMMER
Always wear goggles when using a power trimmer. Keep the blades parallel to the surface and use a wide, sweeping action so that you do not cut into the hedge.

PRUNERS
Formal, large-leaved hedges, such as holly or laurel, should be cut back with pruners to prevent cut leaves from turning brown; make cuts within the hedge to disguise them.

FORMAL OR INFORMAL?

Plants for formal hedges must have a dense habit and tolerate close clipping; the smaller the leaves, the finer textured the surface. Most informal hedges are trimmed in midsummer and autumn. More vigorous species, such as *Chamaecyparis, Crataegus, Lonicera nitida, Ligustrum,* and *Thuja* need trimming in late spring, summer, and autumn. An informal hedge is basically a screen of close-planted shrubs. Trimming depends on flowering and fruiting times, although most need attention only once a year – in spring or after flowering, as for other shrubs.

PLANTS FOR HEDGES

FORMAL	INFORMAL
Boxwood (*Buxus sempervirens*)	Aucuba japonica
	Chaenomeles
Lawson cypress (*Chamaecyparis lawsoniana*)	Hazel (*Corylus*)
	Cotoneaster
	Forsythia
Hornbeam (*Carpinus betulus*)	Garrya elliptica
	Potentilla fruticosa
Beech (*Fagus sylvatica*)	Prunus laurocerasus
Holly (*Ilex*)	Rosa rugosa
Privet (*Ligustrum*)	Tamarix
Lonicera nitida	Tsuga
Yew (*Taxus*)	Weigela

SHAPING A FORMAL HEDGE

Although they often look vertical, formal hedges nearly always have a slight slope, or "batter," to their sides, with the base the widest point. It is structurally strong, less vulnerable to damage by snow or wind, and allows more even distribution of light.

SLOPING SIDES

Sloping sides allow better light penetration to the lower parts of the hedge, so growth is more even from bottom to top. Snow is less likely to damage hedges with sloping sides. Snow should always be brushed upward from the sides to the top to reduce damage.

TAPERED TOP
This shape offers good light penetration and low risk of snow-load damage.

A-SHAPED
The classic shape for formal hedges, it tapers gently to a neat, flat top.

HOW TO USE A SHAPING FRAME

When trimming a hedge, use a taut line as your guide to the top of the hedge. A shaping frame or template – easily made from a piece of plywood – is an invaluable tool when shaping a hedge, especially in its formative years. It gives a precise guide that can be cut to with much greater confidence than can be achieved by eye, especially if you are a novice. It can be discarded once the basic shape has been established and you have gained confidence.

Cut hedge following the line of the template

Taut line stretched horizontally between posts acts as guide when forming a level top

Shaping frame placed over the hedge is moved along as you cut

WOODEN
TEMPLATE

RENOVATING OVERGROWN HEDGES

NEGLECTED AND OVERGROWN HEDGES, with dead patches and bare bases, may be an unwanted inheritance when you move to a new garden, and even well-maintained hedges may gradually edge their way beyond bounds. Ripping out and starting over is an expensive option and removes privacy and shelter. Many hedges, however, respond well to renovation, and it is always worth attempting even if, ultimately, you need to remove and replace.

REDUCING WIDTH

To respond well to renovation, hedge plants must have the ability to regrow from old wood. Some hedge plants, notably conifers (with the exception of yew) do not respond well to severe pruning, and these are almost invariably best replaced. Even with plants that do respond well, it is advisable to deal with the operation over at least two years. Treat one side in the first year, and the other in the second. Reducing height may be better left until the third year. Since you will be removing considerable quantities of living wood, it is essential to fertilize plants well and mulch in spring to aid recovery.

PHASED RENOVATION

Even with plants that tolerate severe pruning, phased renovation offers the best possible chance of success. Allowing at least one growing season for recovery between operations helps avoid overstressing the plants. It is also a good idea to plan ahead: fertilize and mulch well in the season before you begin renovation.

THINNING STEMS
Use loppers and a pruning saw to cut congested, dead, and moribund growth back to the base. New growth from the base ensures good foliage cover from the bottom up.

WHAT TO CUT AND WHEN TO CUT

Evergreen hedges are best renovated in early spring, and deciduous ones when fully dormant in winter. You will need pruners, loppers, a pruning saw, and thick gloves or gauntlets. Taking one side at a time, redefine the new line of the hedge with tall stakes and string. Remove all growth that crosses the line along with dead and congested branches. Start at the base and work to the top. After clearing away weeds and debris, roughen the soil surface with a fork, then apply a dressing of general fertilizer and a mulch of well-rotted organic matter.

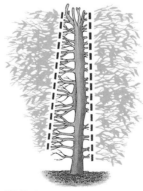

YEAR 1
Cut back one side of the hedge hard in the first year, then trim the other side as usual and at the usual time.

Second side is pruned back in year two

Dense new growth in response to cuts made in first year

YEAR 2
The renovated surface has made dense regrowth. Cut the other side hard by the same amount in the second year.

REDUCING HEIGHT

To recreate a dense, uniform top, reduce the height to at least 6in (15cm) below the desired final height of the hedge. If the upper portions of the hedge are very patchy, be prepared to reduce height even further. If a huge height reduction is necessary to restore the hedge, do this operation in year three of a phased renovation. Use a straight, taut line between tall stakes as a guide to make sure all plants are cut to the same height. Fertilize and mulch well after pruning. It may take one or two seasons before the regrowth disguises the wounds.

LEGGY STEMS
Where the top growth of the hedge is very thin and lanky, steel yourself for some brutal pruning.

A dense, even surface has been restored by severe cutting back

PLANTS THAT RESPOND WELL TO RENOVATION

Hornbeam (*Carpinus*), deciduous. Renovate in late winter or early spring.
Hazel (*Corylus*), deciduous. Renovate in late winter or early spring.
Hawthorn (*Crataegus*), deciduous. Renovate in winter/spring.

Escallonia rubra, evergreen. Renovate in spring.
European beech (*Fagus sylvatica*), deciduous. Renovate in late winter/early spring.
Forsythia, deciduous. Renovate in late winter or early spring.

Holly (*Ilex aquifolium*, *I. opaca*, *I. crenata*), evergreen. Renovate in spring.
Privet (*Ligustrum*), evergreen/deciduous. Renovate in late winter or early spring.
Yew (*Taxus*), evergreen. Renovate in spring.

CONIFER HEDGES

Many conifers make ideal hedges if they are well trained when young and trimmed regularly once established. Green growth and paler-colored young wood usually respond vigorously to trimming. But with few exceptions, such as yew (*Taxus*), conifers are unable to produce new growth from old wood. This leads to problems if they are neglected: they will not resprout if cut back hard into the older, leafless growth, so the only option is replacement.

Young growth is capable of producing new growth when trimmed

Old wood in center will not regrow if cut into

REGULAR TRIMMING

Regular trimming of conifer hedges throughout their lives is essential to maintain a dense surface. If neglected, the usual result is a bare, woody, open center with a fringe of foliage at the extremities. Such hedges are more prone to splitting or collapse in the face of high winds or under heavy snow.

SECTION THROUGH CONIFER HEDGE
The dense outer surface of this hedge disguises a center of old brown wood that is unable to resprout. Only regular trimming will maintain a healthy balance between old and new.

PRUNING AND TRAINING ROSES

AIMS OF PRUNING

WITH ROSES, ASIDE FROM REASONS of good health, the most obvious reason to prune is to maximize the display of their exquisite flowers. The severity (or otherwise) of pruning will influence their numbers, size, and quality. For climbers and ramblers, it can mean training and pruning so that blooms are displayed to best effect near to eye or nose level. It may include deadheading to prolong flowering or, conversely, not deadheading to ensure a display of hips.

TIMING OF PRUNING

There are thousands of roses available, and they are varied in the way they grow. The most important difference in pruning terms is when and how they flower. Many are repeat-flowering or remontant, with some, such as the Hybrid Teas and Floribundas, blooming almost continuously throughout summer. These are pruned in early spring, just before they break into growth. They should also be deadheaded regularly to ensure greater continuity of bloom. Once-flowering roses (that bear their flowers in one flash, usually in early summer) are best pruned as soon as they finish flowering. All roses with tall or whippy stems also benefit from shortening in autumn to avoid wind-rock damage to the roots.

MODERN SHRUB
Renowned for the freedom with which it bears its beautifully scented blooms, the shrub rose 'Graham Thomas' needs only light pruning to maintain its graceful habit.

◀ SWEET RAMBLER *'American Pillar' is an ideal pillar rose, as its name suggests.*

SELECTION AND ROUTINE TASKS

THERE ARE SO MANY HUNDREDS of roses available that selection with regard to color, fragrance, size, and habit is a matter of taste. Some of the loveliest roses bloom only once, but if you want flowers all through the season, choose repeat-flowering (remontant) roses, and be sure to deadhead them regularly and keep them well fertilized. If you prefer to garden with the minimum of chemicals, look for roses that are described as disease resistant.

CHOOSING GOOD PLANTS

Roses are sold as bare-root plants (for planting in the dormant season) or as container-grown plants, which can be planted at any time of year if soil and weather conditions are suitable. Check the roots of bare-root roses for signs of damage or drying out, and make sure they have plenty of fine, fibrous roots. If plants are in leaf, look for glossy foliage that is free from obvious signs of pests and diseases.

Strong shoots arise evenly around stem

Look for a strong bud (graft) union

Look for glossy, healthy leaves of good color

Choose plants with a sturdy, straight, well-staked stem

Good, strong system with healthy fibrous roots

Roots almost fill the clean, evenly moist soil mix

BARE ROOT
Avoid plants with weak top growth; spindly, dried out, or damaged roots; or with a stunted system of scant roots.

CONTAINER-GROWN
Avoid plants with weak shoots, sparse or yellow leaves, signs of pests and diseases, or weeds or moss in the pot.

STANDARD
Avoid plants with weak, crooked stems or uneven top-growth; the head should have strong, evenly spaced shoots.

CUTTING TO A BUD

Roses have alternate buds. When pruning, make a slightly sloping cut about ¼in (5mm) above a a bud on a strong, healthy stem (*see p.14*). Make the cut to a bud that is pointing in the direction you wish the new shoot to grow. Do not leave a long stub (it will die back) and avoid making ragged cuts, which allow diseases to enter easily.

A CLEAN CUT
If the plant is in leaf, use sharp pruners to make an angled cut just above the bud that is visible at the leaf joint.

New growth follows the same direction as the bud is pointing

REMOVING DEAD AND DAMAGED WOOD

Make removing dead, diseased, or damaged wood your first task in pruning roses. If there is a clear demarcation line between live and dead wood, cut to that point to keep the natural barrier intact. If not, cut back dead wood into clean, healthy wood, then shorten crossing stems to a suitable bud. If stems rub against each other, the diseases may enter damaged bark.

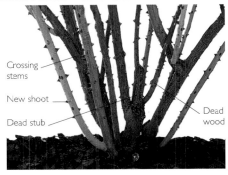

Crossing stems

New shoot

Dead stub

Dead wood

ROUTINE PRUNING
Take out diseased and damaged stems. Take out dead stems and old stubs that have died back and show no signs of new buds, and remove old, unproductive shoots completely. Shorten shoots that cross or rub against each other to a suitable bud or sideshoot.

LESS EQUALS MORE
• Pruning Hybrid Teas and Floribundas hard produces strong growth that bears relatively few, large blooms of excellent quality.
• Pruning them less hard, to strong buds a little higher on the stems, produces more flowers (still of good quality, but slightly smaller) and gives a more natural look.

DEADHEADING

Deadheading removes unsightly faded blooms and prevents the formation of hips, which inhibits further flowers. Snapping spent blooms off between your finger and thumb, just below the swelling beneath the flower, encourages new flowers more quickly than the older technique of cutting dead flowers back to the nearest full-sized leaf. This is because the more foliage is left in place, the better the plant can perform.

OLD METHOD
The fading flower is cut back to the first full-sized leaf. This technique is still useful for summer-pruning once-flowering roses.

NEW METHOD
The swelling beneath the spent flower forms a natural barrier. Snap off dead flowers at this point. This method works especially well on single blooms.

REMOVING SUCKERS

Most rose cultivars are grafted onto a rootstock, which may produce suckers that weaken and eventually take over from the grafted cultivar. A sucker often occurs a short way away from the base of the rose and is usually easily distinguished, because it has leaves different from the grafted plant. If you cut a sucker back to its base, it will be stimulated into vigorous growth. Instead, trace it back to its point of origin, then pull it carefully but cleanly away.

PULLING AWAY
Gently scrape away the soil at the base of the sucker, then trace it back to its point of origin. Wearing thick gloves, grasp it firmly and give a sharp, downward tug to pull the sucker sharply away from the root. Replace the soil.

PRUNING MODERN BUSH ROSES

MOST MODERN BUSH ROSES ARE repeat-flowering, and one of the main aims of pruning them is to ensure a plentiful supply of strong, new shoots, which will bear a succession of flowers throughout summer if deadheaded regularly. The two most important groups, Hybrid Teas and Floribundas, are best pruned back hard each year to a low, open framework of strong stems. In general, other modern bush roses need less severe pruning to give their best.

PRUNING UPON PLANTING

When planting a container-grown bush rose in the growing season, the only pruning it needs is the removal of any spent flowers and damaged growth. Reserve hard pruning until the following spring. All bare-root bush roses, however, are pruned hard right after planting to encourage strong, new growth from low down on the plant.

INITIAL PRUNING
Cut the stems of a newly planted, bare-root bush rose back to outward-facing buds about 3–6in (8–15cm) above ground level to form a low framework of stems.

FLORIBUNDA ROSES

Floribundas, or cluster-flowered bush roses, produce showy masses of flowers in broad, clustered heads throughout summer. During annual spring pruning, if you retain a sufficient length of stem, there will be plenty of buds to develop into flowering shoots. This is the reason why they are not pruned as hard as Hybrid Teas. If the old flowered shoots don't have obvious buds to cut to, simply cut to the desired height. This stimulates dormant buds into growth; any stubs should be trimmed away later.

ESTABLISHED PRUNING
In early spring, cut away all dead shoots and shorten any damaged shoots to strong, healthy buds. Shorten all the remaining stems to about 10–12in (25–30cm) above ground level. Reduce any sideshoots to two or three buds.

A gently sloping cut to an outward-facing bud keeps the center of the bush open. Leave only strong stems with plenty of promising buds

Cut out old, dead, and weak shoots back to healthy wood at the base

Cut back any strong sideshoots to 2–3 buds from the main stem; the topmost bud should point in the desired direction of growth

GOOD CHOICES

Amber Queen
Angel Face
Cherish
French Lace
Europeana
Eyepaint
First Edition
Iceberg
Impatient
Memento
Playboy
Playgirl
Scentimental
Sexy Rexy
Sunsprite

HYBRID TEA ROSES

Hybrid Teas, or large-flowered bush
roses, bear large flowers either singly or
in clusters of three on stiff, upright stems.
Once established, hard pruning will ensure
the production of strong flowering stems
that bloom throughout summer.

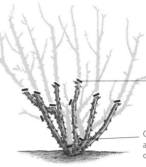

Shorten strong,
healthy stems
to an outward-
facing bud

Cut dead, diseased,
and crossing stems
out at the base

GOOD CHOICES

Dainty Bess	Opulence
Double Delight	Peace
Fragrant Cloud	Sheer Elegance
Midas Touch	Touch of Class
Mister Lincoln	Valencia

ESTABLISHED PRUNING
*In early spring, prune back hard to leave a
framework of 4–5 strong stems at 8–9in
(20–23cm) above ground level.*

PATIO AND MINIATURE ROSES

These two groups are more compact,
scaled-down versions of Hybrid Teas and
Floribundas and are pruned at the same
time and in a similar way, but less severely.
If regularly deadheaded, most will also
flower all summer long some even
blooming until the first frosts.

ESTABLISHED PRUNING
*Since bush size varies, it is hard to
prescribe the height of cut; as
a general rule, reduce the
height by about one third.*

Shorten the main
stems, being sure
to remove all of
the previous
season's flowers

Shorten sideshoots
to within 2–3 buds
of main stems to
reduce congestion

Cut out oldest stems and
dead, diseased, damaged,
and crossing wood

GOOD CHOICES

Fairhope	Popcorn
Jean Kenneally	Rise 'n' Shine
Little Bo-Peep	Starina
Magic Carrousel	Stars 'n' Stripes
Minnie Pearl	Sweet Dream

GROUNDCOVER ROSES

Groundcover roses come in two main types.
Shrubby ones need only light trimming to
shorten any overly long stems and to
reduce sideshoots if the center of the bush
becomes congested. Trailing ones may just

need to be kept within bounds. Simply cut
to an upward-facing bud or shoot. Prune
repeat-flowering groundcover roses in early
spring and once-flowering ones after
flowering in midsummer.

CONTAIN THE SPREAD
*If trailing stems
encroach on other
nearby plants, cut
them back to an
upward-facing bud or
sideshoot in spring or
after flowering.*

GOOD CHOICES

Bonica	Rosy Cushion
Flower Carpet	Snow Carpet
Grouse	Suma
Kent	Surrey
Red Blanket	Swany

MODERN SHRUB AND OLD ROSES

MODERN SHRUB ROSES ARE A diverse group. Mostly larger than bush roses and often repeat flowering, a few bear flowers in one midsummer flush. They develop their full grace and stature with light annual pruning. Most Old roses bloom in a glorious summer flush of often highly scented blooms. Both groups need only light pruning upon planting; simply shorten any overlong shoots that spoil their outline, and remove damaged or dead shoots.

MODERN SHRUB ROSES

Most modern shrubs grow to 4–6ft (1.2–2m) tall by as much across and combine vigorous growth with repeat flowering. These are best pruned lightly in early spring, as shown below. Use the same technique for modern shrubs that flower once, but do so just after flowering.

Some modern shrubs are taller versions of Hybrid Tea and Floribunda roses (*see p.58–59*) and are pruned in a similar way in early spring, except that the main stems are shortened by only one-third to maintain stature, and sideshoots are reduced to two or three buds to improve flower quality.

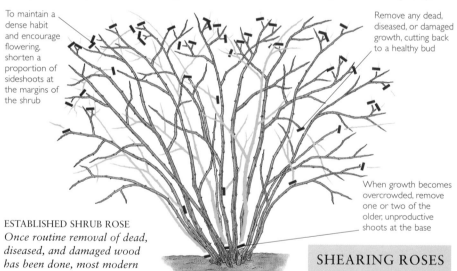

To maintain a dense habit and encourage flowering, shorten a proportion of sideshoots at the margins of the shrub

Remove any dead, diseased, or damaged growth, cutting back to a healthy bud

When growth becomes overcrowded, remove one or two of the older, unproductive shoots at the base

ESTABLISHED SHRUB ROSE
Once routine removal of dead, diseased, and damaged wood has been done, most modern shrubs need only light pruning.

GOOD CHOICES

Agnes	Francine Austin	Morden Centennial
Ballerina	Fritz Nobis	Nevada
Buff Beauty	Gertrude Jekyll	Penelope
Carefree Beauty	Golden Wings	Sharifa Asma
Chinatown	Graham Thomas	The Fairy
Constance Spry	Heritage	Westerland
Felicia	L.D Braithwaite	Yesterday

SHEARING ROSES

• The more robust shrub roses, such as the Rugosas, especially when grown as a hedge, can be sheared with power hedge trimmers.
• Modern bush roses, when grown in massed formal beds, can also be sheared. It may, however, leave dead growth within the bushes. For best results, this should be removed with pruners.

OLD ROSES

There are several groups of Old roses that, once established, are pruned in one of the two ways outlined here Pruning needs vary according to whether their habit of growth is dense and upright (as with the Gallica roses) or more open and spreading (in the Alba, Bourbon, Centifolia, China, Damask, Moss, and Portland roses). Most of the Old roses flower once and are pruned as soon as the summer flush of flowers is over. The repeat-flowering Old roses, such as the Bourbons and Chinas, are pruned in early spring and deadheaded throughout the season; these may bloom until hard frost.

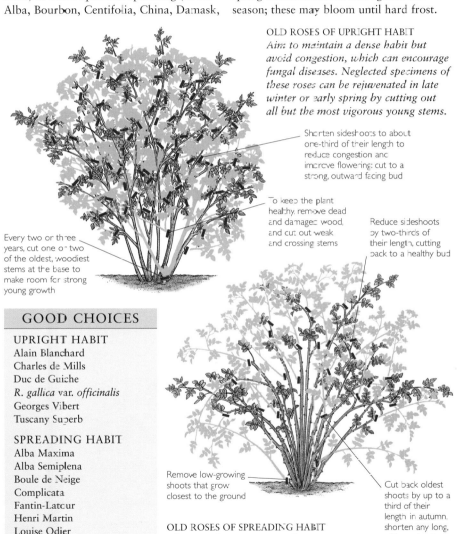

OLD ROSES OF UPRIGHT HABIT
Aim to maintain a dense habit but avoid congestion, which can encourage fungal diseases. Neglected specimens of these roses can be rejuvenated in late winter or early spring by cutting out all but the most vigorous young stems.

Shorten sideshoots to about one-third of their length to reduce congestion and improve flowering: cut to a strong, outward facing bud

To keep the plant healthy, remove dead and damaged wood, and cut out weak and crossing stems

Reduce sideshoots by two-thirds of their length, cutting back to a healthy bud

Every two or three years, cut one or two of the oldest, woodiest stems at the base to make room for strong young growth

GOOD CHOICES

UPRIGHT HABIT
Alain Blanchard
Charles de Mills
Duc de Guiche
R. gallica var. officinalis
Georges Vibert
Tuscany Superb

SPREADING HABIT
Alba Maxima
Alba Semiplena
Boule de Neige
Complicata
Fantin-Latour
Henri Martin
Louise Odier
Madame Plantier
Maiden's Blush
R. × odorata Mutabilis

Remove low-growing shoots that grow closest to the ground

Cut back oldest shoots by up to a third of their length in autumn, shorten any long, whippy shoots to prevent wind-rock and damage to the crown and roots

OLD ROSES OF SPREADING HABIT
The aim of pruning is to relieve congestion and renew flowering shoots. To rejuvenate neglected shrubs, remove all but the strongest young shoots, and shorten them by a third.

CLIMBING AND RAMBLING ROSES

ONE OF THE SIMPLEST WAYS OF TRAINING climbing and rambling roses is on a vertical wall or fence. It works best if the rose stems are trained on strong horizontal wires, set at least 2in (5cm) away from the vertical surface to allow good air circulation, which minimizes fungal diseases. Using this method, stems are readily accessible both for pruning and for releasing or adjusting ties as the rose grows and as old stems are removed and replaced with younger ones.

WALL-TRAINED CLIMBERS

Climbing roses have stiff, upright growth and flower repeatedly on sideshoots arising from a framework of older wood. They are sold with longer shoots than bush roses. Do not prune them upon planting; it removes the buds needed to make new shoots. In year one, just take out dead wood and prune tips to encourage branching. Train and tie stems in as they grow, spacing them evenly to achieve good cover of the support.

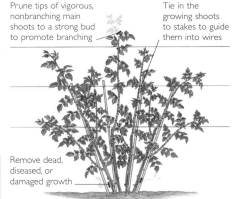

Prune tips of vigorous, nonbranching main shoots to a strong bud to promote branching

Tie in the growing shoots to stakes to guide them into wires

Remove dead, diseased, or damaged growth

PLANTING AND TRAINING, YEAR ONE
Put guide wires in place; the bottom one 18in (45cm) above ground, subsequent ones about 12in (30cm) apart. Plant climbers 18in (45cm) away from the base of the wall.

HORIZONTAL RULES

With both rambling and climbing roses, training stems to as near to the horizontal as possible encourages the production of more flowering sideshoots than if left to grow upward (*see p.10–11*). Careful placement of stems can ensure that an entire vertical surface is covered in bloom from top to bottom.

WALL-TRAINED RAMBLERS

Upon planting, prune all stems back to about 18in (40cm) above ground level to promote strong new growth. Fan the new shoots out and tie them in to their support as they grow, keeping as near to the horizontal as possible. Ramblers have long, flexible stems and bear their single flush of flowers most freely on year-old wood. Most produce new shoots freely from the base. When established, take out one in three of the old, flowered shoots at the base after flowering to encourage new ones. Ramblers will flower perfectly well on the same wood for several years, but if you need to reduce the plant's size, you can cut back all flowered shoots.

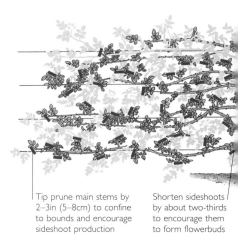

Tip prune main stems by 2–3in (5–8cm) to confine to bounds and encourage sideshoot production

Shorten sideshoots by about two-thirds to encourage them to form flowerbuds

PRUNING ESTABLISHED CLIMBERS

Climbers are mainly repeat-flowering and are pruned when dormant. Pruning in late autumn reduces the risk of long stems being whipped about by winter winds.

Once the rose has filled its allotted space, pruning aims to renew the older framework branches by cutting back less productive flowered shoots to a lower new shoot or strong bud. To encourage the flowered sideshoots to produce new flowering shoots the following year, they are shortened by two-thirds of their length or to two or three buds. At maturity, you can cut out any old, unproductive shoots at the base to stimulate new growth low down on the plant.

GOOD CHOICES

Aloha	Danse du Feu
Altissimo	Fellemberg
America	Handel
Berries 'n' Cream	New Dawn
Climbing Iceberg	Parade
Compassion	Sympathie

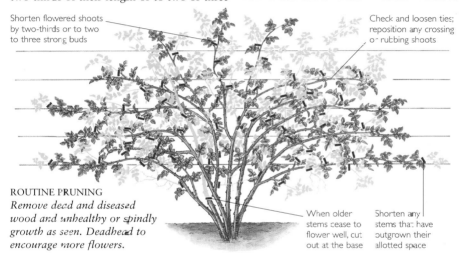

Shorten flowered shoots by two-thirds or to two to three strong buds

Check and loosen ties; reposition any crossing or rubbing shoots

ROUTINE PRUNING
Remove dead and diseased wood and unhealthy or spindly growth as seen. Deadhead to encourage more flowers.

When older stems cease to flower well, cut out at the base

Shorten any stems that have outgrown their allotted space

Cut one in three flowered shoots to the base; take out in sections to avoid damaging remaining stems

ROUTINE PRUNING
The main aim of pruning is to ensure regular replacement of old shoots with new ones that will flower more freely.

SMALL RAMBLERS

The following are more restrained ramblers good for smaller spaces:
Albertine
Bleu Magenta
Crimson Shower
Flora
Goldfinch
Little Rambler
Paul Transon
Princesse Louise
Sander's White Rambler
Spectabilis
Veilchenblau

SUPPORTS FOR CLIMBING PLANTS

TRAINING CLIMBERS (including climbing and rambling roses) onto upright supports is an ideal way of bringing a vertical element to a garden's design. Match the vigor of the plant to its supporting structure so that it will cover it without overwhelming it. If the plant is very vigorous and you think you may need to restrict its size, make sure that it tolerates hard pruning. To give plants a firm hold, you may need to furnish support with wires, netting, or a trellis.

PILLARS AND PERGOLAS

There are two ways of training on pillars or pergolas. Straight up gives a top canopy to a pergola more rapidly. Spiraling stems around pillars ensures flowers on the pillar and over crossbeams of a pergola. Plant about 10in (25cm) from the pillar base and guide the new growth to the top on wires or a trellis. As stems reach the crossbeams, train and tie them out along them.

Stems cling more easily to wires and grow upward much more rapidly to the top of the support than if twined around it

Twining plants can attach themselves more easily to system of wires running up the sturdy uprights of a pergola or a pillar

PLANTS FOR PERGOLAS

ROSES	CLIMBERS
Alister Stella Gray	*Actinidia polygama*
American Pillar	*Akebia quinata*
City of York	*Clematis* (many)
Excelsa	*Jasminum officinale*
Lawrence Johnston	*Lonicera* (many)
Maigold	*Schisandra rubriflora*
Phyllis Bide	*Vitis coignetiae*
Seagull	*Wisterias* (all)

INITIAL TRAINING
Some plants, such as the twiner shown here, will try to twine around any support they come into contact with. Most are best given the initial guidance of additional wires.

Permanent main stem is trained horizontally beneath the beam

Wires stretched tautly between the cross beams provided strong support for the main stems

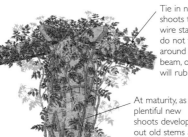

Tie in new shoots to wire staples; do not twine around the beam, or they will rub

At maturity, as plentiful new shoots develop, cut out old stems at the base, in sections

ROSE PRUNING ON A PERGOLA
Tie in growing shoots to wires or staples as they grow. Deadhead if practical. Climbers need no regular pruning. Prune ramblers to encourage new basal growth (see p.62–63).

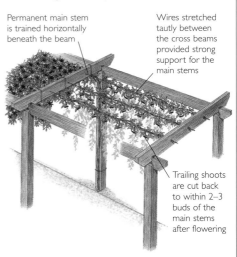

Trailing shoots are cut back to within 2–3 buds of the main stems after flowering

PERGOLA-TRAINED PASSIONFLOWER
Once the main stems reach the top of the pergola, they are trained along horizontal wires so that the flowering shoots hang down to display the flowers to great advantage.

TRIPODS AND ARCHES

Any climber with flexible stems can be grown on an arch or tripod, provided that vigor is matched to the size and sturdiness of the structure. Tripods are an excellent way to train stems to the horizontal to create vertical features clothed with bloom. When training on arches, plant on the outside of both sides of the arch; it is very difficult to train stems downward. It is also best to avoid thorny-stemmed plants.

Shorten overly long shoots to a strong bud below the top, and cut flowered shoots to a lower, outward-facing bud

Cut some old stems back to young replacement shoots, and tie them in as they grow to fill gaps

TRIPOD TRAINING
Spiral young, flexible stems around the support, then tie them in. Prune roses as when wall-training (see p.62–63); shorten flowered sideshoots and cut oldest stems back to encourage replacements.

GROWING ON AN ARCH
Prune overly long shoots to maintain the arch's form. Foliage plants can be trimmed at any time. Prune flowering plants according to their individual needs, or flowering will be impaired.

Plastic netting on frame gives clinging stems firm support

Shorten shoots as necessary to keep passageway clear

PLANTS FOR TRIPODS AND ARCHES

ROSES		CLIMBERS	
Alba Semiplena	Gloire de Dijon	Actinidia kolomikta	Jasminum officinale
Alchymist	Graham Thomas	Clematis (many)	Lonicera (many)
Boule de Neige	Handel	Eccremocarpus scaber	Passiflora caerulea
Constance Spry	Reine Victoria	Humulus lupulus	Solanum crispum
Dortmund	Summer Wine	'Aureus'	Trachelospermum
Dublin Bay	Swan Lake	Jasminum beesianum	jasminoides
	Warm Welcome		Wisteria

TRAINING CLIMBERS UP A HOST TREE

Make sure the host plant is vigorous, well-established, healthy, and able to support the weight of the chosen climber. If you plant too close to the host, the climber may struggle to grow well. If possible, plant at the perimeter of the canopy of the host and on the side of the prevailing wind. The stems will make their way to the sunnier side of the host. Provide thick rope, wire, or netting to guide the climber to its host.

FORMATIVE TRAINING
Careful siting and early guiding in of stems to the lower branches are vital; later, stems scramble naturally toward the light.

Protect branch fork with sheath of rubber hose on supporting rope

CLIMBERS AND WALL SHRUBS

AIMS OF PRUNING

WHEN GROWING IN THE WILD, climbing plants concentrate all of their energy into growing upward as rapidly as possible, scrambling over other plants and obstacles toward the light, flowering only when they reach their goal. In gardens, pruning and training are usually essential to shape, direct, and sometimes to control growth so that the ornamental features are displayed where they can be readily enjoyed, rather than at the top of their support.

TYPES OF CLIMBER

Climbers support themselves in various ways on their upward quest: by their tendrils, adhesive pads, or aerial roots, or they may twine around their support. The way they climb does not affect the way in which they are pruned, but it does affect the type of support they need. An ivy, for example, can cling to and climb up a bare stone wall or tree trunk by its aerial roots, but a twining honeysuckle or tendriled clematis needs guiding onto wires or a trellis before it can climb. Shrubs with no climbing adaptations can be trained on a wall but will always need training and tying in to their supports. It's important to match the vigor of the climber to its support, both to ensure full cover and to avoid overwhelming the support.

EXTRA WARMTH
*Although uncommon, wall training is ideal for rosemary (*Rosmarinus officinalis*); this Mediterranean native enjoys the drier soil at the base of a wall and flowers freely as it basks in the wall's reflected warmth.*

◀ DELIGHTFUL DUO *The vigor and growth habit of clematis and wisterias are ideal for pergolas.*

CHOOSING A CLIMBER

ONE OF THE MOST IMPORTANT THINGS to check when selecting a climber is that its potential height and spread will fit into the space you have allotted to it. If you need to constantly prune it back hard to confine it to bounds, not only do you risk compromising the full glory of the ornamental features for which it was chosen, such as flowers or fruit, but you are also making some unnecessary hard work for yourself.

BUYING GOOD PLANTS

Climbing plants are usually grown and sold in containers. The top-growth should consist of a well-balanced set of strong, healthy, and undamaged shoots. If buying deciduous plants when dormant, look for plenty of healthy buds on the stems. Check for evidence of pest infestation or diseases, looking above and beneath the leaves.

Check that the soil mix is evenly moist and that its surface is free of weeds and mosses. The soil mix should be full of well-developed, pale-colored, living roots, but not so full that the roots coil around the inside of the pot. Turn the pot over: if there are young root tips just visible at the drainage holes, the plant is well rooted.

Healthy foliage of good color on vigorous, sturdy stems

Plant is clearly labeled; good labels also give size of plant and pruning tips

WHAT TO AVOID
• Don't buy plants with weak, spindly stems and dead or damaged buds.
• Avoid potbound plants with congested roots coiled within the pot or with masses of root protruding through the drainage holes.
• Avoid plants with obvious signs of pests or diseases.

Check that ties are secure but loose enough not to cut or constrict the stems

Healthy new buds low down on the plant

Roots are plentiful, visibly healthy, and not coiled or congested

WELL-FORMED PLANT
This plant has plenty of sturdy, well-supported stems, healthy young leaves, and fat new buds at the base. The surface of the soil mix is free of weeds and moss.

STRONG, HEALTHY ROOTS
This plant has a mass of pale-colored, living roots distributed evenly within the pot; dead roots are usually brown and look soggy. There is no sign of coiling or constriction.

INITIAL TRAINING OF CLIMBERS

All climbers that climb by tendrils, twining stems, or hooked thorns need some sort of support to cling to; whether you provide a trellis, wires, or netting, this should be put in place before planting. Even vigorous climbers need guiding to their support at first, including self-clingers (see box, below), at least until they become self-supporting. The main aim of early pruning and training is to develop a strong framework of main branches that will provide good coverage of the support.

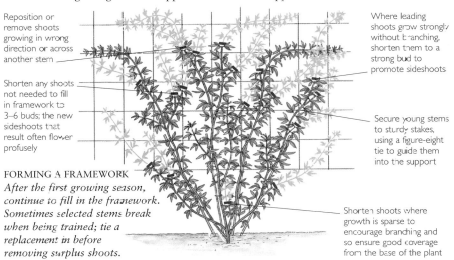

Reposition or remove shoots growing in wrong direction or across another stem

Shorten any shoots not needed to fill in framework to 3–6 buds; the new sideshoots that result often flower profusely

Where leading shoots grow strongly without branching, shorten them to a strong bud to promote sideshoots

Secure young stems to sturdy stakes, using a figure-eight tie to guide them into the support

FORMING A FRAMEWORK
After the first growing season, continue to fill in the framework. Sometimes selected stems break when being trained; tie a replacement in before removing surplus shoots.

Shorten shoots where growth is sparse to encourage branching and so ensure good coverage from the base of the plant

SELF-SUPPORTING CLIMBERS

Hedera helix, (English ivy), *H. canariensis*, and *H. colchica* cling by means of adhesive stem roots; they do no harm to sound brickwork but may dislodge old mortar.

Hydrangea anomala subsp. *petiolaris* climbs using aerial roots; they may take two or three seasons to begin attaching. *Parthenocissus* have suckering pads that make thinning established specimens difficult. Plants are vigorous, so allow plenty of space. *Schizophragma integrifolium* uses aerial roots that cling best on rough surfaces.

GUIDING AND TYING IN

Guiding and tying in is essential to direct growth and to encourage good coverage of the support. Fan the stems out across the support so that the stems grow right across the support, rather than right up the middle. Always try to train some shoots to as near horizontal as possible to encourage sideshoots. Young shoots are often fragile, so work with great care.

GUIDING IN
Stems of twining and tendril plants are guided carefully into the support while still young and flexible.

TYING IN
A figure-eight tie secures the stem but allows for stem expansion and buffers the stem against a hard surface.

PRUNING ESTABLISHED CLIMBERS

SOME CLIMBERS NEED LITTLE FURTHER ATTENTION once they have been trained and pruned in their early years to cover the available space. These are the ones to choose for places where access may be difficult – high on a wall or in the branches of a tree. On others, you may just need to remove dead, damaged, or diseased wood and to take out old growth to stimulate replacement shoots, but pruning to enhance flowering is often an annual or twice-yearly task.

ROUTINE TASKS

Dead, damaged, and diseased wood should be removed when seen. Deadheading will improve subsequent flowering and should be done wherever practical. Congestion and crossing growth is difficult to avoid on vigorous climbers, such as *Clematis montana*, but thinning flowered shoots each year will help. Otherwise, shear them back to their support every three or four years. If a permanent framework of woody stems has been developed, shortening excess growth regularly will avoid a tangled buildup.

DEAD WOOD
This jasmine stem has died back to buds that have produced healthy young shoots, so it is safe to assume that a natural barrier has formed to isolate the dead wood.

Cut back to just beyond the visible barrier between living and dead wood

New growth at the base of the dead flower stalk

DEADHEADING
If practical, remove unsightly dead stalks or flowerheads to improve appearance and later flowering; take care not to damage new growth.

The flowered shoot is cut back to a strong new shoot

Vigorous replacement shoot will flower next season

THINNING GROWTH
Thin spent flower shoots to prolong flowering or improve next year's display; it also helps prevent congestion.

TRACING STEMS
When thinning, tracing stems is not easy. Cut a stem at the base, then later cut and tease out the growth that wilts.

SHEARING DENSE CLIMBERS
Shearing dense climbers may be the only practical option, but do it at the right time for the individual plant.

MAINTENANCE PRUNING

Climbers trained against a wall or other support need annual pruning if they are to remain healthy and in good shape. As the plant matures, it is necessary to prune out some old wood to restrict size or encourage new growth to maintain good coverage. Most flowering or fruiting climbers also need pruning to keep them productive. The degree of pruning needed depends on the individual plant, its vigor, and condition.

DORMANT SEASON PRUNING
Timing of pruning varies but the principle is the same. Guide and tie in new shoots or reposition young stems to fill gaps in the framework. Check and readjust ties as necessary.

Remove weak, congested, and crossing stems, and shorten overly long stems back to a strong bud. Tie new growth in to fill gaps

Cut out dead, diseased, damaged, and unproductive old stems at their base

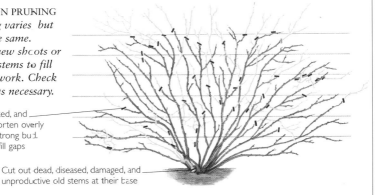

RENOVATION PRUNING

Overgrown and neglected climbers full of tangled woody growth are difficult to retrain, but basically sound plants can be renovated in the dormant season. If the plant is diseased or has died back extensively, it is best to replace it. The easiest way is to cut the entire plant back to the base and start again, provided the plant will tolerate drastic pruning. If it will not stand hard pruning or you can't wait for it to grow back, renovate over two to three years.

WHEN TO PRUNE

Early-flowering plants: usually flower on the previous season's wood before midsummer and are pruned immediately after flowering.

Late-flowering plants: flower on the current season's wood and, like deciduous climbers grown for foliage, are pruned when dormant.

Evergreens: are often most safely pruned in early summer to avoid damage by frost to resulting soft new growth. New growth quickly disguises cut marks.

Cut out dead, diseased, and damaged wood and remove all debris from behind the support

Tie in strong new growth to fill gaps in the framework, and shorten sideshoots

STAGED RENOVATION
Over 2–3 years, cut back one in three of the oldest stems to ground level each year. Old stems are are easier to remove if cut into sections first. Tease out the old growth and tie in the new.

Cut back one in three of the old stems to the base

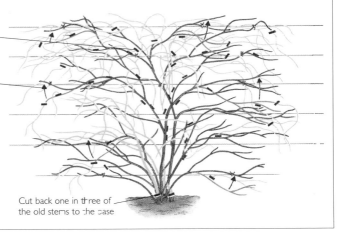

WALL-TRAINED SHRUBS

MANY SHRUBS CAN BE TRAINED on vertical surfaces to enhance the display of their flowers of their flowers or fruits. Wall training is especially useful in small gardens, where there may be insufficient space for these often large shrubs to be grown as free-standing specimens. Walls give some protection against winter cold, so it is also useful in cooler climates for shrubs that are not totally hardy, and the additional warmth will enhance flowering in hardy shrubs, too.

INITIAL TRAINING OF WALL SHRUBS

Install wire or a trellis for support, with a space of about 2in (5cm) between the wall and support to allow good air circulation. Plant wall shrubs at least 18in (45cm) from the base of the wall to avoid the dry soil caused by the "rainshadow" effect of the wall. Cut single-stemmed specimens back hard to encourage branching, then select 4–5 strong stems and tie them in as they grow to form a well-spaced framework.

GOOD FOR WALLS

Chaenomeles: prune after the spring flowering as for pyracanthas.
Cytisus battandieri : prune after flowering in summer to replace older framework branches occasionally.
Forsythia suspensa: shorten flowered shoots after flowering in early spring.
Fremontodendron: just shorten outward-growing shoots in midsummer after the first flush of flowers.

INITIAL WALL TRAINING
Tie in main stems to the support, and then space out and tie in strong sideshoots. Shorten inward- and outward-facing shoots to 1–2 buds to induce sideways branching.

Shorten long sideshoots by a few buds to stimulate branching, then tie resulting shoots into the framework

Remove or shorten low-growing shoots that cannot be tied in or that grow the wrong direction

ESTABLISHED PRUNING

All wall shrubs share these requirements, although timing of pruning varies according to flowering time. Tie in new shoots as they grow, and check all ties regularly to avoid constriction. Shorten or remove shoots growing into or away from the wall. Tie in sideshoots to fill gaps. Aim to replace old stems with vigorous new ones over time.

Shorten weak stems to stimulate strong growth; shorten shoots at limits of allotted space

Prune flowered growth at the correct time; cut back, if necessary, to relieve congestion

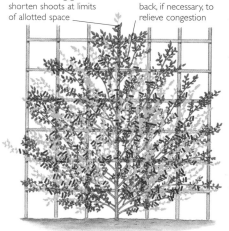

PRUNING AN ESTABLISHED WALL SHRUB
At maturity, remove older, less productive growth to make way for younger shoots. Continue to tie in new growth, and reduce inward- or outward-facing shoots to 1–2 buds.

PRUNING PYRACANTHAS

Pyracanthas are grown for their clusters of early summer flowers and for the bright berries that follow. They are borne on short sideshoots, or spurs, that develop on old wood. The main pruning – shortening the main shoots and outward-growing shoots to encourage production of flowering spurs – is done in midspring. In late summer, the flowered shoots are shortened to two to three leaves to expose the ripening berries.

Shorten vigorous new sideshoots to 2–3 buds in midspring to encourage the formation of flowering shoots

Cut back fruit-bearing sideshoots by 2–3 leaves after flowering, to display the ripening clusters of berries

Remove completely any weak, dead, damaged or unhealthy shoots

WALL TRAINING
Once a permanent framework of woody branches has been established, cut back outward-growing shoots and shorten other shoots in midspring.

Tie in strong new shoots as they grow to fill any gaps in the framework

PRUNING WINTER JASMINE

This sprawling plant does not cling and always needs tying in to its support if wall grown. It bears masses of tiny yellow flowers in winter and early spring and is pruned immediately after flowering. Cut back all flowered shoots to within two or three buds of the main framework. Large plants can be clipped back with hand shears.

KEEP IT NEAT

If not pruned annually, the vigorous winter jasmine, *Jasminum nudiflorum*, produces new growth that mounds up over older growth, leading to a messy buildup of old wood. It tolerates hard pruning; keeping it pruned back close to its support ensures dense, neat growth that will be covered with flowers.

BUILDING A FRAMEWORK
Cut back all shoots by up to two-thirds of their length upon planting, and tie in the resulting new shoots evenly across the support to achieve good coverage.

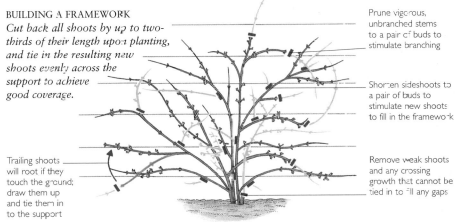

Prune vigorous, unbranched stems to a pair of buds to stimulate branching

Shorten sideshoots to a pair of buds to stimulate new shoots to fill in the framework

Trailing shoots will root if they touch the ground; draw them up and tie them in to the support

Remove weak shoots and any crossing growth that cannot be tied in to fill any gaps

PRUNING CLEMATIS

THE CORRECT PRUNING OF CLEMATIS is a source of confusion, but the system shown here is very logical. All clematis fall into one of three groups, depending on the flowering season and the age of the wood on which flowers are borne. Initial training is the same for all groups: cut to low buds, or pinch out the young shoot tips, upon planting. Provide the support of wires or a trellis, and tie in young stems to the support; they are brittle, so take care not to snap them.

GROUP 1 CLEMATIS

This group includes the early-flowering species and their cultivars that flower early in the year (between late winter and early spring) on the previous year's mature wood. These are generally robust and vigorous plants, often used to cover large walls, buildings, and large trees. They are pruned immediately after flowering; once established, they usually need pruning only if overgrown. Cut back overly long shoots to pairs of healthy buds. Remove frost-damaged shoots only when danger of further frost has passed. Old, congested plants can be thinned if necessary or, if total renovation is needed, all stems can be cut back almost to the base.

PRUNING GROUPS

Group 1 plants: *C. alpina* and cultivars, *C. armandii*, *C. cirrhosa*, *C. macropetala* and cultivars, *C. montana* and cultivars.

Group 2 plants: 'Barbara Dibley', 'Barbara Jackman', 'Belle of Woking', 'Carnaby', 'Daniel Deronda', 'Duchess of Edinburgh', 'General Sikorski', 'H.F. Young', 'Lasurstern', 'Nelly Moser', 'Niobe', 'Proteus', 'Richard Pennell', 'The President', 'Vyvyan Pennell', 'W.E. Gladstone', 'William Kennett'.

Group 3 plants: 'Abundance', 'Bill MacKenzie', 'Etoile Violette', 'Graveteye Beauty', 'Mme. Julia de Correvon', *C. orientalis*, 'Polish Spirit', *C. rehderiana*, *C. tangutica*, *C. tibetana*, *C. viticella*.

Clematis 'Gipsy Queen', 'Hagley Hybrid' and 'Jackmanii' can be pruned as Grp 2 or Grp 3.

GROUP 1 PRUNING
Needs minimal pruning.
Immediately after flowering, cut
back overly long shoots and, if necessary,
thin crowded growth.

Thin if growth is too dense, cutting out selected shoots at their point of origin or to strong buds

Shorten overly long shoots to strong buds. Cut weak or damaged shoots to strong buds at their base

GROUP 2 CLEMATIS

These are the large-flowered hybrids that flower in late spring and early summer on the previous year's wood and again (later in summer) on the current season's growth. They are pruned in the dormant season, in late winter or early spring before new growth begins. You can stagger pruning by cutting back some shoots later than others to further prolong flowering. Or, you can prune them as for Group One, then cut them back to the base every 3–4 years to give one late, glorious display of flowers.

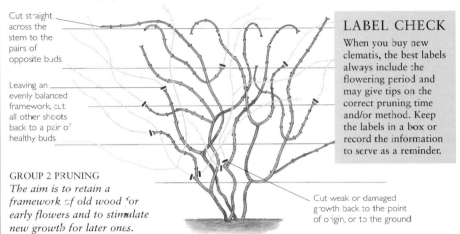

Cut straight across the stem to the pairs of opposite buds

Leaving an evenly balanced framework, cut all other shoots back to a pair of healthy buds

GROUP 2 PRUNING
The aim is to retain a framework of old wood for early flowers and to stimulate new growth for later ones.

Cut weak or damaged growth back to the point of origin, or to the ground

LABEL CHECK

When you buy new clematis, the best labels always include the flowering period and may give tips on the correct pruning time and/or method. Keep the labels in a box or record the information to serve as a reminder.

GROUP 3 CLEMATIS

The late-flowering species and hybrids flower late in summer and autumn on the current season's growth. They make new growth from the base each year and so are cut back hard in late winter or early spring when buds show signs of new growth. This makes them very useful and easy to manage when growing through other plants (such as roses) to prolong their hosts' season of interest. Established plants require hard pruning annually; without it, vigor and flowering performance dwindle.

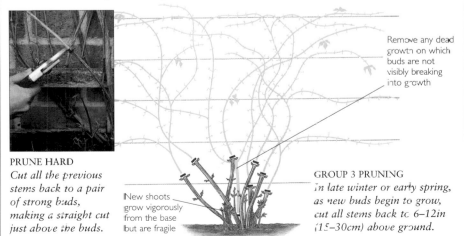

Remove any dead growth on which buds are not visibly breaking into growth

PRUNE HARD
Cut all the previous stems back to a pair of strong buds, making a straight cut just above the buds.

New shoots grow vigorously from the base but are fragile

GROUP 3 PRUNING
In late winter or early spring, as new buds begin to grow, cut all stems back to 6–12in (15–30cm) above ground.

PRUNING WISTERIA

WISTERIAS IN FULL BLOOM are one of the glories of spring and early summer, but if incorrectly or insufficiently pruned can make a wild tangle of stems with few visible flowers. They flower from clusters of buds on sideshoots arising from old wood and are pruned twice a year, in winter and in summer, about two months after flowering. It takes three or more years to build up a framework in espalier form, which is one of the best ways of displaying the hanging flowers.

YEAR 1

Put a system of strong wires in place, the lowest 18in (45cm) above ground level, the remainder 12in (30cm) apart. As the main shoot grows, tie it vertically to the wires. Select two strong sideshoots, then tie them in at a 45° angle.

PRUNING UPON PLANTING
Cut back the main shoot to about 30in (75cm) above the topmost sideshoots; do not cut below the graft union.

Attach the main shoot to a stake tied to the wires

Remove all sideshoots to stimulate strong, upward growth

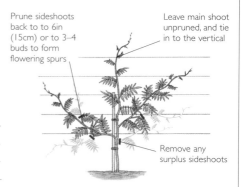

Prune sideshoots back to to 6in (15cm) or to 3–4 buds to form flowering spurs

Leave main shoot unpruned, and tie in to the vertical

Remove any surplus sideshoots

SUMMER PRUNING, YEAR 1
The aim is to begin forming a strong framework and to begin encouraging the formation of flowering spurs on sideshoots.

YEAR 2

Begin a program of winter and summer pruning, aiming to encourage further upward growth of the main shoot and to create more tiers of permanent framework branches that will bear flowers in later years.

WINTER PRUNING, YEAR 2
Cut back the main shoot to 30in (75cm) above the topmost sideshoots, and lower and tie in last season's sideshoots to the horizontal.

Sideshoots previously trained at 45° are bent to the horizontal; prune them back by a third of their length

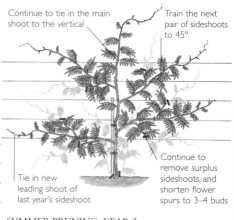

Continue to tie in the main shoot to the vertical

Train the next pair of sideshoots to 45°

Tie in new leading shoot of last year's sideshoot

Continue to remove surplus sideshoots, and shorten flower spurs to 3–4 buds

SUMMER PRUNING, YEAR 2
Continue developing the tiers of sideshoots, and shorten the sideshoots or flowering spurs that arise from them to 3–4 buds.

YEAR 3, WINTER

Continue pruning to create more tiers of sideshoots until the space is filled. Each winter, cut the main shoot back by about 30in (75cm) above the topmost sideshoots, and lower the previous season's sideshoots to the horizontal, shortening them by about a third of their length. Check ties, and loosen any that constrict the stems.

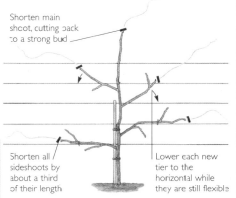

Shorten main shoot, cutting back to a strong bud

Shorten all sideshoots by about a third of their length

Lower each new tier to the horizontal while they are still flexible

WINTER PRUNING IN THE THIRD YEAR
You are continuing to develop a strong framework by shortening the main shoot and sideshoots back into mature wood.

GET THE BEST FLOWERS

• Wisterias may take several years to begin flowering, so be patient.
• It is best to choose named cultivars, which will be grafted plants of good flower quality.
• Wisterias on nitrogen-rich soils produce a great deal of leafy growth at the expense of flowers. Do not apply high-nitrogen fertilizers.

PRUNING ESTABLISHED WISTERIAS

Wisterias are long-lived plants, so effort put into the early training to a good form will be repaid by many decades of flowers. They seldom need renovation, but if they do, it is best done in stages over several years. Remove one main sidebranch at a time, in winter, and train in a replacement. If wall maintenance becomes necessary, the plant can be cut to the base. It will resprout rapidly, and training can begin again. It will take several years for such a hard-pruned plant to resume flowering, however.

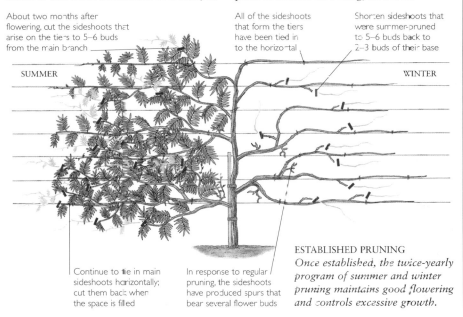

About two months after flowering, cut the sideshoots that arise on the tiers to 5–6 buds from the main branch

All of the sideshoots that form the tiers have been tied in to the horizontal

Shorten sideshoots that were summer-pruned to 5–6 buds back to 2–3 buds of their base

SUMMER

WINTER

Continue to tie in main sideshoots horizontally; cut them back when the space is filled

In response to regular pruning, the sideshoots have produced spurs that bear several flower buds

ESTABLISHED PRUNING
Once established, the twice-yearly program of summer and winter pruning maintains good flowering and controls excessive growth.

INDEX

ACKNOWLEDGMENTS

Picture Research Samantha Nunn
DK Picture Library Richard Dabb, Hayley Smith
Index Hilary Bird

Dorling Kindersley would like to thank:
All staff at the RHS, in particular Barbara Haynes, Simon Maughan and Susanne Mitchell; Dean Peckett, Senior Supervisor in the Floral Department at the RHS Garden, Wisley.

American Horticultural Society
To learn more about the work of the Society, visit AHS on the internet at **www.ahs.org** or call 1-800-777-7931.

Photography
The publisher would like to thank the following for their kind permission to reproduce their photographs:
(key: b=bottom, c=center, r=right)
2: Photos Horticultural; 4: Photos Horticultural (bc); 5: Photos Horticultural (bc); 6: Eric Crichton Photos; 7: Clive Nichols; 8: Photos Horticultural (br); 18: Eric Crichton Photos; 19: Harry Smith Collection; 34: Harry Smith Collection; 35: Photos Horticultural; 54: Harry Smith Collection; 55: Photos Horticultural; 66: Photos Horticultural; 67: Photos Horticultural.

All other images © Dorling Kindersley.
www.dkimages.com